Essential Virtual Reality *fast*

D1003125

Springer

London
Berlin
Heidelberg
New York
Barcelona
Budapest
Hong Kong
Milan
Paris
Santa Clara
Singapore
Tokyo

John Vince

Essential Virtual Reality *fast*

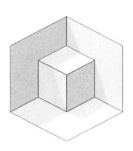

How to Understand the Techniques and Potential of Virtual Reality

 Springer

John Vince, MTech, PhD, FBCS, CEng
The National Center for Computer Animation, Bournemouth University,
Talbot Campus, Poole, Dorset, BH12 5BB, UK

ISBN 1-85233-012-0 Springer-Verlag London Berlin Heidelberg

British Library Cataloguing in Publication Data
Vince, John, 1941-
   Essential virtual reality fast : how to understand the
   techniques and potential of virtual reality
   1.Virtual reality
   I.Title
   006
   ISBN 1852330120

Library of Congress Cataloging-in-Publication Data
Vince, John (John A.)
   Essential virtual reality fast : how to understand the techniques
   and potential of virtual reality / John Vince.
      p.   cm.
   Includes index.
   ISBN 1-85233-012-0 (paperback : alk. paper)
   1. Human-computer interaction. 2. Virtual reality. 3. Computer
   graphics. 4. Three-dimensional display systems.   I. Title.
   QA76.9.H85V52   1998
   006--dc21   98-22387

© Springer-Verlag London Limited 1998
Printed in Great Britain
2nd printing 1999
3rd printing 2001

Typesetting: from author's electronic files
Printed and bound by the Creative Print & Design Group (Wales), Ebbw Vale
34/3830-5432   Printed on acid-free paper   SPIN 10792463

Contents

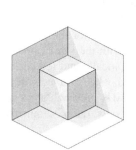

1
What is Virtual Reality?

Introduction

During the last decade the word *virtual* became one of the most exposed words in the English language. Today, we have *virtual* universities, *virtual* offices, *virtual* pets, *virtual* graveyards, *virtual* exhibitions, *virtual* wind tunnels, *virtual* actors, *virtual* studios, *virtual* museums, *virtual* doctors—and all because of *virtual* reality.

Virtual Reality (VR) hit the headlines in the mid-1980s, and spawned a series of conferences, exhibitions, television programs, and philosophical debates about the meaning of reality. And overnight, everything suddenly had a virtual dimension—from shopping to sex!

What is virtual reality?

Such public enthusiasm for a new technology was totally unexpected, but was not wasted by the VR industry, who were more than keen to exploit every printed word and televised image about their product. At VR exhibitions long queues of inquisitive people would form to discover what it would be like to experience an immersive computer-generated world. Five minutes, though, was more than enough to convince the would-be cyber citizen that the reality of VR was mostly virtual. The virtual worlds were not as enthralling as had been promised, and something called 'lag' meant that the displayed images were not always in synch with head movements. Although there was some disappointment with these embryonic systems, it was clear that, with time, the technology had an exciting future. Today, VR has evolved into a variety of configurations based upon head-mounted displays, PCs, workstations, immersive rooms, large screen systems, and virtual tables.

Early VR systems described a computer technology that enabled a user to look through a special display called a Head-Mounted Display (HMD)—and instead of seeing the normal world, they saw a computer-generated world. One of the perceived advantages of this approach was the way it integrated the user with the virtual images. To begin with, the user's head movements are monitored electronically and fed back to the computer creating the images, so that as the user moves their head, objects in the scene remain stationary—just as they do in real life. Most HMDs prevent the wearer from seeing the real world, which, together with a stereoscopic view, quickly immerses them in the substitute world.

There is a natural temptation to reach out and touch virtual objects, even though they do not exist. And this is where VR offers something new—it does allow the user to reach out and move objects about, as if they existed. Just how this is achieved will be described later, but for now, let us assume that it is possible.

If it were possible to build a system that enabled a user to move about a virtual world and interact with it, then it would have extraordinary applications. It would be possible to go on virtual holidays, test drive virtual cars, and even interact with virtual actors in 3D television. Car designers could design concept cars and explore them at a virtual level long before they were ever built. Surgeons could practice operations on virtual cadavers, and master delicate maneuvers before performing a real operation. The applications are limitless—but it all hinges on whether it is possible to build such systems, and what our expectations are.

But VR is much more than immersive systems working with a HMD, and we will discuss such systems throughout this book.

Who should read this book?

As soon as VR became established as a major area of study, a number of books surfaced on the subject covering everything from how to build a VR system in your garage, to what the virtual world would be like in the year 2050. As VR matured, further books appeared addressing hardware and software issues, and the research effort that would be needed to make VR really happen.

Today, VR is moving very quickly and there is an ever increasing population wanting to know more about this exciting subject, but do not necessarily want to know too much about the underlying mathematical techniques. If you fall into this category, then this book is for you.

The aims and objectives of this book

The aim of this book is to take the lid off VR and describe exactly what it is about—and I will attempt to achieve this without using any mathematical notation. There are other excellent books that address this aspect of VR.

My objectives are many: After reading this book you should be able to understand the principles behind a typical VR system. You should be able to develop some of these principles into the design of new VR systems. You will understand the jargon used within VR; and you will be able to communicate to VR specialists any personal requirements you may have for your own VR system. No doubt there will be some readers who will want to delve deeper into the mathematics, 3D geometry and the software used in VR, and this book will provide that first step towards this exciting subject.

In this book I will explain the origins of VR; how it works; and how VR is being used. I will also provide you with a snapshot of today's VR systems, and what steps you will have to take to implement your own system. After reading the book you should have a good understanding of what VR is, and what it is not.

Assumptions made in this book

I have not made very many assumptions about you, the reader. Basically, I assume that you understand what a computer is and how it works. You probably already know that computers can be used to create images. Perhaps you have already seen such images in recent films such as *Titanic* containing amazing computer-generated special effects. You may even have experienced a VR system, or seen television programs about VR. But also I am hoping that you are eager to learn more about how the technology works and how it is being applied.

How to use the book

The book has been designed to be read from cover to cover. Each chapter covers concepts and techniques that are developed in subsequent chapters. But obviously where the reader feels that they already are familiar with the subject of a chapter, then simply jump ahead.

Some VR concepts and terms

A typical dictionary definition of the word *virtual* is "*being something in effect but not in actual name or form*"—and the words *virtual reality* conjure up a vision of a reality without requiring the physical nuts and bolts, or whatever else is needed to build that reality.

What we refer to as *reality* is based upon something we call the *external physical world*. This universe—whatever it is—can only be explored by our senses, and we learn from an early age to describe our experiences in terms of color, sound, temperature, smell, taste, touch, etc. Therefore, a *virtual* reality seems to suggest a reality that is believable, and yet does not physically exist. But what do we mean by *believable*? Well *believe* means "*to accept as real or true*". But for how long could we be deceived by an alternate reality? One second? One minute? One hour? Furthermore, what do we mean by *true*?

Immediately one senses this pedantic approach to defining the words 'virtual reality' is leading us nowhere, fast. This, too, became very evident to followers of VR in the early days of the technology. And it soon became apparent, that computers could not, at the time, create virtual worlds that were as believable as the real world. Nor can they today, although some systems are coming close.

During the 1990s the terms *Virtual Environments* (VE) and *synthetic environments* emerged. And although the term virtual reality has persisted—for it always grabs the headlines—there is a general acceptance that virtual reality is about creating acceptable substitutes for real objects or environments, and is *not* really about constructing imaginary worlds that are indistinguishable from the real world.

Navigation and interaction

Basically, VR is about using computers to create images of 3D scenes with which one can navigate and interact. By navigate we imply the ability to move around and explore features of a 3D scene such as a building; whilst interact implies the ability to select and move objects in a scene, such as a chair.

In order to navigate and interact we require real-time graphics, which implies fast computers. Navigating and interacting with the real world has certain advantages if we are equipped with stereoscopic sight, and the same advantages are realized if our computer-generated images are also stereoscopic. Naturally, such a demand puts an even higher requirement upon a computer's processing capability.

Immersion and presence

In 1965 Ivan Sutherland published a paper "The Ultimate Display" (Sutherland, 1965) that described how one day, the computer would provide a window into virtual worlds. In 1968 he built a head-mounted display that presented to the user left and right views of a computer-generated 3D scene, such that when the user's head moved, the virtual scene remained stationary. The images were far from life like—they were simple line drawings. But as they were stereoscopic the user perceived an impression of looking at a solid 3D object. Virtual Reality was born.

Unfortunately, the 1960s and 1970s was not a period renowned for low-cost, fast computers and consequently VR remained dormant. In the 1980s real-time computer graphics became a reality, and VR became a commercial reality. Initially, early VR systems comprised a real-time computer system, a head-mounted display, and an interactive glove. Apart from supplying the user with stereoscopic images, the HMD immersed the user in the virtual world by preventing them from seeing the real world. Immersion increased the sensation of presence within the virtual world, and for some people, immersion distinguished VR systems from other types of real-time computer graphics systems. For this community, a VR system had to provide a user with a 'first-person' view of the virtual world. Looking at a workstation screen was not virtual reality—it was just fast computer graphics!

Immersive and non-immersive VR

During the 1990s everyone relaxed their earlier rigid views about what comprised a VR system, and accepted a wider definition for VR. PC systems emerged capable of displaying real-time images of 3D environments that could be navigated and support interaction, and also they could be configured to support a HMD. Obviously, they were a VR system—but not as powerful as their more expensive partners.

The technology of HMDs has taken much longer to perfect than many people had anticipated. There has also been some resistance to using HMDs over long periods of time. They can be tiring, and some people just do not like the sensation of being visually isolated from their surroundings. This has meant that in some applications, the advantages of VR have had to be appreciated using a mix of immersive and non-immersive techniques. Virtual prototyping using CAD is one such application.

Now this has caused many to rethink just what is VR. Does a VR system have to have a HMD? Can a VR system be nothing more than a PC fitted with an appropriate graphics board? Or can VR be any computer-based system that supports the navigation and interaction with a 3D environment? In an attempt to answer these questions it may be useful to consider those techniques that should not be considered as virtual reality.

What is not VR?

Ever since it was realized that computers could be used to create images, the subject of computer graphics has evolved further and been applied to almost every aspect of graphic design. Today, computer-generated graphics are found in desktop publishing systems, data visualization systems, computer games, television programs, flight simulators, and behind some of the most amazing special effects in films. But are they all VR? Well this question is open to dispute.

Take, for example, computer games. Although the first computer games operated in real time, the graphics were 2D, and in no way could be considered as virtual reality. Today, computer games are 3D and provide an incredible variety of scenarios. One can fly fighter planes over realistic terrain; drive sports cars around recognizable grand prix circuits; and test one's skills as a special agent fighting a similar foreign agent. Just take a look at the recent Nintendo game *GoldenEye* by Rare Ltd. Such games definitely employ the elements of 3D navigation and interaction, and I am quite happy to embrace them as virtual reality systems. Computer games technology is evolving very fast, and games systems will probably become a major sector of VR.

But what about film special effects? Today, most films contain some form of computer-generated special effects, but they cannot be considered as VR. To begin with, the actors are not aware of the virtual characters, such as dinosaurs, passengers on the Titanic, or alien creatures. Actors are directed to look towards where a synthetic character is supposed to be, and act appropriately. Then at the post-production stage, the live action is integrated with the computer-generated elements to produce the final film.

At no time during the making of the film do the actors see their virtual cast or virtual environments. They are unable to navigate virtual worlds, and cannot undertake any form of interaction.

Film special effects companies have produced some truly amazing computer-generated scenarios, but they are not VR—they are excellent examples of computer animation, which is another subject!

For example, the image shown in Plate 1 is computer generated and depicts a ground vehicle and spacecraft flying over Mars sometime in the next century. The terrain is based upon real Martian data and the vehicle follows every undulation in the ground leaving behind a realistic dust track. Although everything is virtual, there is no computer available today capable of running the rendering software in real time. If we assume that this image took approximately 10 minutes to render on a workstation, we could produce 6 images an hour. But in a VR system we require something in the order of 20 per second! Which means that there is a speed factor of 12,000 between the two systems. Therefore, we will have to wait a very long time before it is possible to simulate such scenarios in real time.

The Internet

In recent years the Internet has exploded into existence and promises to transform the way governments govern, companies trade, and even the way ordinary individuals interact with one another. Although the Internet was used initially to communicate text and 2D graphics, it was soon realized that it could be used to process 3D computer graphics. Almost overnight VRML (Virtual Reality Modeling Language) appeared and enabled Internet browsers to interact with 3D environments.

VRML is a language for modeling objects and environments using very simple commands, which can be downloaded as a VRML file over the Internet. With the aid of a suitable browser, the VRML descriptions are interpreted locally to create an image. Special instructions are available to support animation interaction and navigation, which, as we have seen, are the general features of a VR system.

Although VRML models and environments are still very simple, there is no reason why they should not eventually be able to support very sophisticated designs. However, whilst we wait for these developments, the Internet is perceived to be a powerful medium for VR. And there is every chance it will develop into a major sector for future VR work.

We will take a look at VRML in Chapter 6 to learn a little about the language syntax, examples of models and potential applications.

Summary

In this chapter I have attempted to give a brief overview of what VR is about, and we have seen that navigation, interaction, immersion and presence are characteristics of VR systems. The term VR is also mistakenly being associated with processes that are definitely not VR, especially in the field of film special effects. Basically, a VR system uses real-time computer graphics in such a way to make the user believe that they are part of a virtual domain. This can be achieved using a HMD, hand-held BOOM display, CAVE, virtual table, dome or large screen based system. But not everyone has access to such technology and PCs and workstations play a major role in screen-based VR systems.

In the end however, it is not up to me or anyone else to dictate what VR should or should not be. We must be prepared to accept that VR technology will undergo dramatic developments during the next few years, and what we currently accept as VR could disappear and be replaced by something equally revolutionary. For the moment though, I will continue with the above definition and proceed to explore the essential elements of VR.

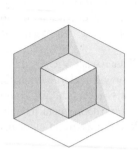

2
The Benefits of Virtual Reality

Introduction

Although we live in an age where we can buy things that serve no purpose what so ever, most products have to provide a service and offer real benefits. In industry, it would be unthinkable to employ any technique or technology that did not add value in some form or another. For example, once upon a time, computers were more trouble than they were worth. They were unreliable, software was problematical, and if one could get by without using them, then that was the preferred course of action.

Today, it would be unthinkable for any company not to consider using computers. Even though computers will 'crash' occasionally, and software collapses regularly, their advantages are enormous. And as industry embraces the Internet and adjusts to the concept of global markets, the age of digital communication is here to stay. But when a revolutionary technology such as VR comes along, it is only natural that industry reacts with caution.

A first and natural reaction was to ask searching questions about cost, performance, life cycles, upgrades, training, software availability, benefits, etc. Unfortunately, ten years ago when VR systems were just emerging, the answers to these questions were vague and not very inspiring. VR companies were hoping that some industrial sectors would share their own vision of VR, and take a similar gamble. Failure would not destroy the company, but success promised real rewards.

Fortunately, some companies did accept the challenge of VR. And as one might have expected, some projects failed, but others prospered, and today, such projects have identified clear and viable markets for VR.

My personal opinion at the time was that it would be unthinkable for any company to suddenly embrace a new technology and adopt new and unproved methods and procedures. VR was so revolutionary that the only way for it to be accepted was that it should complement rather than replace any existing process. For example, one special application for VR is in the CAD industry, where 3D components and assemblies are already being designed at a virtual level. VR could not have replaced the workstation approach to CAD. To begin with, the software was not available, nor could the systems handle large CAD databases. However, what VR could do was to provide a valuable simulation and visualization environment for evaluating CAD models. Today, this is developing into a prosperous sector for VR. Fig. 2.1 shows an exploded view of an assembly that can be viewed in real time from any point of view. By activating the virtual VCR controls the individual components move to show how the assembly is constructed.

Fig. 2.1 Exploded view of a CAD database. (Image courtesy of Division)

3D visualization

We have all become accustomed to working with computers using monitors or LCD screens. They have been with us for so long that it is hard to imagine any other way or working without computers. But it is equally hard to imagine that we will be using screens 50 or a 100 years from now. There has to be new technological developments that will completely transform this user interface.

For the moment, though, traditional computer graphic systems display images of 3D scenes upon the flat screen of a monitor. Even though the scenes may be very realistic, we are aware that we are looking at a 2D image, when perhaps, we should be looking at a 3D scene. It is still a question of us, the viewer, looking at the computer holding the image.

Immersive VR transforms all of this by making the user part of the virtual environment. A HMD or CAVE provides the wearer with a 'first-person' view of the virtual scene and effectively places the user next to, or inside the virtual object. We know from experience the value of seeing and touching something, rather than looking at a photograph.

A photograph of a car may be very accurate and realistic, but nothing can replace the sense of scale, proportion, color, and visual impact of being next to a real car. Simply by walking around a car we can take in subtle changes in its surface geometry. We notice how highlights travel along body panels, and how concave features are blended with convex features. We notice the relationship of the interior to the exterior, and how one blends into the other.

Fig. 2.2 A virtual car visualized inside a VR system.
(Image courtesy of Division)

There are myriad reasons why a flat image is inferior to a 3D view of a solid object, which is why VR offers so much to 3D visualization. The key question however, is what value does one place upon being able to see a virtual design in 3D as shown Fig. 2.2, rather than 2D?

If designers can get by without using HMDs and VR, then so be it. But the same could have been said about replacing traditional engineering drawing with CAD systems. Yes it was possible to get by without CAD, but it was also impossible to progress without CAD. CAD systems have transformed the way we design digital processors, cars, planes, rockets, satellites, offshore platforms, etc., and many of these structures would have been impossible to build without the help of computers.

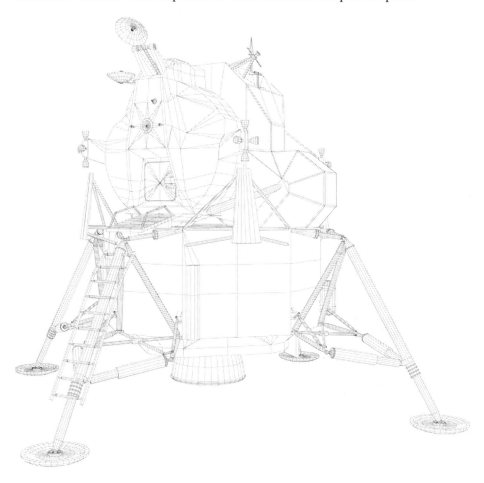

***Fig. 2.3** Moon Lander. (Image courtesy of Viewpoint DataLabs)*

We could not have landed on the moon without computers and CAD. And as we prepare to colonize planets within our solar system, CAD models such as the one shown in Fig. 2.3 are being used to visualize future space missions and the construction of space cities.

CAD also plays a vital role in the design of chemical plants whose complexity defies the imagination (Fig. 2.4). Such structures would be impossible to build without computers and today's sophisticated software tools. And as this complexity increases, we will require even more sophisticated tools for visualizing these structures.

On a much smaller scale, take, for example, the problem of designing a car wheel (Fig. 2.5). Prior to the days of CAD, it would have taken an experienced draftsperson many hours of work creating detailed orthographic projections of the curved features.

Today, with the benefit of CAD, it can be designed in a fraction of the time, and also visualized as a 3D object. But VR takes us one step further; with VR it is possible to see a set of wheels attached to a virtual car, and inspect the car from any point of view in real time.

Fig. 2.4 *External and internal visualization of a chemical plant.*
(Images courtesy of Virtual Presence)

It is highly likely that today's CAD systems will become tomorrow's VR systems. And already one can see how the benefits of visualization offered by VR are being integrated into the CAD methodology. However, this does not imply that future CAD designers will be wearing HMDs. They may still translate their ideas into concepts using screens of some sort, but they will also rely upon projection systems, as well as HMDs to view their designs.

Fig. 2.5 A car wheel modeled on a PC using Lightwave. (Image courtesy James Hans)

Another thing to bear in mind is that where VR attempts to make the user part of the virtual domain, other 3D technologies are under development that make 3D virtual objects part of the real world. For example, 3D television sets already exist in research labs, and other forms of 3D computer displays are being developed. And it is highly likely that in the near future it will be possible to display realistic views of virtual objects that can be manipulated directly by our hands and fingers.

Navigation

Immersive VR

It was mentioned in Chapter 1 that navigation and interaction are important features of a VR system. In immersive VR, navigation is made possible by tracking the position of the user's head in three dimensions, such that when they move forward, they pass by objects that are no longer in front of them. And when they turn their head, they see those objects that were beyond their field of view. We take such phenomena for granted in the real world—it just happens naturally.

However, there is a problem if the user wishes to walk about the virtual world, especially if it's rather large. To begin with, a cable connects the user's HMD to the computer, which may only extend to 3 or 4 meters. Secondly, the head tracking technology that may only operate over a short radius of 2 to 3 meters also restricts the user's mobility.

But all is not lost. It is possible to navigate a virtual environment without physically moving. All that is necessary is to instruct the host computer to 'fly' towards a certain direction, as instructed by the user. Such instructions are communicated via a hand-held 3D mouse. The direction is often determined by the user's gaze direction. For example, if the user is looking along a virtual corridor, simply by pressing a mouse button, the user will apparently drift along the corridor until giving a 'stop' instruction. By gazing in another direction and issuing the 'fly' command, the user can navigate the maze of corridors without their feet ever leaving the ground.

Similar instructions can be used to ascend and descend flights of stairs. Which means that it is possible to move about virtual houses, submarines, oil platforms, cities, offices, chemical refineries, nuclear power stations, and any other structure stored in the computer. Effective though this may be, it does create problems for those people who are sensitive to motion sickness—but more of this later.

Fig. 2.6. Spaceball by Spacetec. Spacestick by Virtual Presence. Spacemouse by Logitech. (Images courtesyof Spacetec, Virtual Presence, and Logitech)

Desktop VR

So far we have only looked at navigation using immersive VR. Non-immersive or desktop VR systems must be navigated using totally different techniques.

Somehow we need to communicate to the host software how we wish to move in 3D space. For example, we may wish to go forward, backward, left, right, up or down. But we may also require to stand still and rotate, left or right, or look up or down. Now in an immersive system this can be achieved through head movements, but without a 3D tracker other hardware or special interface tools are required.

One solution is to use a joystick or a 3D mouse as shown in Fig. 2.6. These devices can communicate three directions of translation and rotations about three axes. But without such useful physical devices we must resort to some virtual subterfuge. An approach that has been successful with Web browsers is to use two or three screen controls that work in conjunction with a conventional 2D mouse.

Fig. 2.7 3D Webmaster's navigation controls.

Fig. 2.7 shows the screen buttons used in Superscape's 3D Webmaster. The button on the left controls the translating movements left, right, up and down. The center button controls moving forwards, backwards, turning left and right; and the button on the right is responsible for tilting downwards and upwards. Simply by clicking on one of these buttons and moving the mouse in an appropriate direction one can navigate with ease through complex 3D VEs.

To be able to navigate without physically moving opens up an extraordinary range of applications for VR. It implies that one could explore an architect's plans for a house and visualize what would be seen from different rooms. A trainee marine could learn about the interior of a submarine using a VR system, so that when he or she arrived at the real submarine, they would be familiar with different compartments and their access points, and how to operate relevant controls. Personnel expecting to be transferred to an oil platform could learn about the site's emergency procedures using a VR system before being posted. It would be possible to become familiar with foreign cities, new office structures, chemical refineries, long before they were ever built.

For example, Fig. 2.8 shows an image from a VR project where a control room for British Nuclear Fuels Ltd. (BNFL) was modeled at a virtual level using Superscape's VRT system. The scene shows the room with desks, chairs, monitors and other displays. Operators were able to familiarize themselves with the room long before it was built. And at this virtual level it was possible to evaluate seating plans, the visibility of critical displays, inter-operator communication, and other ergonomic issues.

Fig. 2.8 *A BNFL control room modeled using Superscape's VRT system.*
(Image courtesy of Virtual Presence)

Interaction

Initially the idea of interacting with virtual objects seems impossible. But it is something we take for granted when working with a word processor. For example, in writing this book I have been continually cutting text and moving it to a different place. 'Cut and paste' is a technique used extensively throughout software packages. It saves incredible amounts of time and makes computers just a little more user-friendly.

If we can cut and paste in 2D, it should be possible to perform the same operation in 3D. In 2D we use a mouse to mark the text to be cut, and the cursor position to mark the place to paste. We require a similar process in 3D to identify the object we wish to cut, together with its new position.

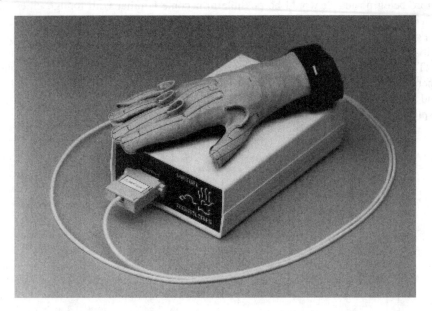

Fig. 2.9 CyberGlove. (Image courtesy of Virtual Technologies)

Immersive VR

One of the first devices to aid interaction was the interactive glove. When worn by the user its position in space and finger positions are relayed to the host computer. These signals are used to control the position of a virtual hand, and the orientation of its virtual fingers, which the user sees in their HMD. Thus as the user moves their real hand about in space they see the virtual hand duplicate the same movements—delayed slightly by a fraction of second.

Meanwhile, inside the host computer, the geometry of the virtual hand is adjusting to the position of the user's real hand. And as this geometry is defined numerically (more about this later), it can be compared by the host software to see if any of the hand's features collide with the geometry describing the virtual environment, which also has a numerical basis. Fortunately, modern computers can perform these numerical comparisons with great speed, and may only require a few thousandths of a second to undertake this task on a small database. When a collision or interference is detected between the virtual hand and a virtual object, the host software reacts by coloring the object red, for example.

The user will see this change in color as confirmation that a collision has been recognized. The host computer now requires a separate signal to confirm that the selected object is to be moved. On receiving this signal, the virtual object is effectively joined to the user's virtual hand. And wherever the user moves their real hand, the object moves with it. When a new place is identified for the object—which can be anywhere, even hanging in space—another signal is given to release it from the user's grasp. Fig. 2.9 illustrates the CyberGlove manufactured by Virtual Technologies. It employs 2 bend sensors on each finger, and other sensors to monitor thumb crossover, palm arch, wrist flexion and wrist abduction (bending away from the central axis).

Desktop VR

Interacting with virtual objects on a desktop system is slightly different, but equally easy and effective. For example, in Superscape's DO 3D system one positions the screen cursor over the required object and presses the mouse's left-hand button. The system responds by displaying the object's boundary box. Then, by pressing the mouse's right-hand button, the object can be dragged to a new position. The top image in Fig. 2.10 shows a greenhouse that has been selected with the left-hand mouse button. And the image below shows how the greenhouse has been dragged to a new position using the mouse's right-hand button.

The ramifications of interacting with VEs are enormous, for it implies that one can interact with and modify the status of any virtual environment. As a trivial example, one could play immersive chess; walking around the board picking up the chess pieces, and then waiting for the computer's response. What such an exercise would achieve is questionable, but the principle is sound. On a higher note, one could experiment with assembling a collection of virtual engineering components to ensure they could be fitted together correctly. And perhaps in an architectural application, an architect could interactively position walls, doors and windows to explore optimum layouts.

The examples are endless and support the concept of undertaking anything from servicing an airplane engine to the intricacies of virtual surgery. We will explore more of these applications later on.

Physical simulation

I have mentioned that the user's hand and the database for the virtual environment have a numerical basis, which will be explained in detail in the next chapter. But if numbers are the basis of the virtual environment one cannot expect virtual objects to mimic accurately their physical counterparts. For instance, in the real world when I drop a glass on a hard floor, the glass breaks into an unpredictable number of pieces. It would be too much to expect a virtual glass to behave in the same way if it were dropped. In fact, a virtual glass would not drop if it were let go. It would remain in the position it was released. Virtual objects require virtual gravity if they are to be subject to an accelerated fall!

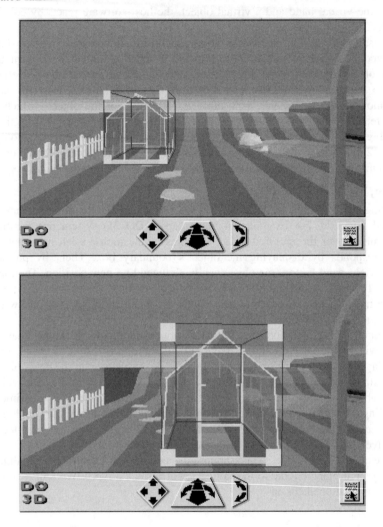

Fig. 2.10 *Object selection and translation using a conventional mouse.*

But if we implement virtual gravity, what happens when the virtual glass collides with the virtual floor? Nothing—it simply passes through the floor and falls towards the center of the virtual world. It only stops falling when the VR software is reinitialized. However, if we want the glass to recognize the floor as a solid object, and explode into a thousand pieces, which in turn fall to the floor, we have a problem. Such exercises require sophisticated simulation software to subject virtual objects to physical forces. It can be done—but not in real time, and therefore not within modern VR systems.

Expecting a VR system to simulate an exploding glass is asking too much of today's technology, but other physical behaviors could be simulated. For example, a ball could be dropped and allowed to bounce. A chair on wheels could be pushed against a wall and a simulated bounce created. A piece of virtual flesh could be pulled to explore its elastic properties. It could also be cut in two to mimic a surgical maneuver.

The real problem with simulation is the computational power required evaluating the mathematical equations describing the physical process. If such digital horsepower can be provided by an appropriate supercomputer, without degrading the performance of the VR system, then it is possible to simulate some very sophisticated behaviors.

If behaviors are required for effect rather than physical accuracy, then it is possible to compute in advance an animated sequence of objects. For example, when our virtual glass hits a virtual floor, an animation sequence can be played showing individual glass fragments twisting and tumbling in space. It will look very realistic, but it will look the same whenever we drop a glass!

Simulation, then, is possible, but we cannot reproduce the level of detail that occurs in the real world. We will *never* (a very dangerous word to use) be able to experience a virtual beach where virtual bathers are playing in the virtual sea, splashing with virtual waves, whilst virtual palm trees swing in a virtual breeze. We will *never* be able to simulate this with the same fidelity of the real world. We could not even approach it. However, it could be simulated if we lowered our expectations.

Virtual environments

Early flight simulators employed scale models of airports upon which trainee pilots acquired flying skills, and experienced pilots were evaluated every six months. The models had many disadvantages. To begin with, they were physically large (typically 50 m^2). They required skilled people to build them; they required substantial levels of illumination; they were static, and could not show any moving features, such as ground vehicles; they could not reproduce different weather conditions; and furthermore, an airline would require a separate model for every specific airport.

When a pilot was using the simulator, a small video camera would move over the model and relay back to a screen in front of the pilot what was seen from that position in space. The effect was acceptable, but required a significant amount of physical technology. Today, pilots train in simulators using virtual models of airports. Although they still require skilled modelers to construct the numeric database, the models take up no physical space, for they are stored on a computer disk. They require no illumination, for virtual illumination models are used to simulate different times of the day and year. Features of the virtual environment can be animated, such as cars driving along freeways, ground vehicles moving about terminal buildings, and other aircraft landing and taking off. VEs are available for every major international airport, and copies only take a few minutes to create. And virtual fog, rain, snow, thunder and lightning can be introduced at the press of a button.

Fig. 2.11 shows an image produced by a real-time image generator manufactured by Evans & Sutherland. It depicts a countryside scene with undulating terrain, trees, cornfields, and dramatic clouds. What is amazing is that it only takes a few thousandths of a second to produce!

Fig. 2.11 *Real-time, 3D image of terrain. (Image courtesy of Evans & Sutherland Computer Corporation, Salt Lake City, Utah, USA)*

Fig. 2.12 shows a Boeing 737-800 flight simulator manufactured by Thomson Training & Simulation. The curved structure at the top houses the panoramic mirror that reflects the computer-generated images into the cockpit, and immerses the pilot and co-pilot inside the virtual environment. Because they are unable to see the outside world, they have no external cues to help them understand their orientation. Therefore, the motion platform shown supporting the simulator, can be used to lean the simulator back to create the sensation of acceleration, or lean forward to create the sensation of deceleration.

All of the computers, including the image generators, are located away from the simulator to keep the moving mass to a minimum. But even then, the platform still weighs several tonnes, and very powerful hydraulic pumps are required to move it in real time.

Architects have always relied upon physical models to provide a realistic impression of the finished project. Such models are very expensive to construct, and once built, offer few advantages. It is impossible to navigate the models internally, although small video cameras are often maneuvered into small corridors to convey interior views. The obvious next step for architects is to embrace VR technology, together with all of its advantages.

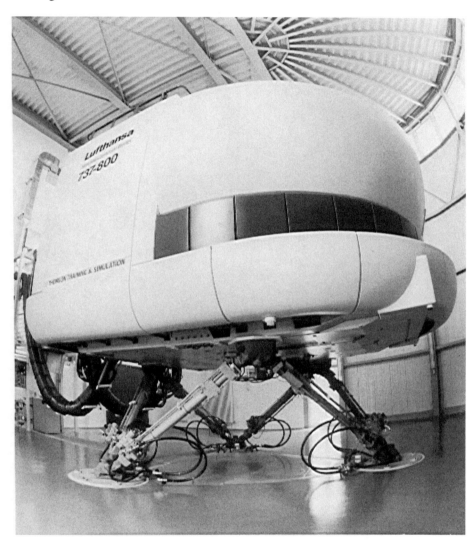

Fig. 2.12 *A Boeing 737-800 full flight simulator for Lufthansa.*
(Image courtesy of Thomson Training & Simulation)

The designers of Chartres cathedral for example, only had access to muscle power and primitive mechanical tools, which is why it took many decades to construct. No doubt they employed elevations, projections, and perhaps crude models, but they were unable to visualize the grandeur of the final building. Today, we can store the cathedral's geometry within a computer (Fig. 2.13) and explore it at a virtual level.

Fig. 2.13 *Chartres cathedral. (Image courtesy of Viewpoint DataLabs)*

Modern architects now have access to the most sophisticated design aids ever invented, making it possible to construct buildings of great complexity, and build them within very short time spans. Furthermore, modern software is capable of incredible realism making it possible to simulate with great accuracy complex lighting conditions. Fig. 2.14 and Plates 5 and 6 show the extraordinary level of photo-realism that is possible using modern radiosity renderers.

Fig. 2.14 *Radiosity view of an interior using the LightWorks rendering system. (Image courtesy of LightWork Design)*

Manufacturers of submarines go to extraordinary lengths to ensure that the final submarine can be operated successfully and efficiently. Often a scale model of a submarine is constructed and evaluated using suitably scaled mannequins representing sailors. Obviously this is an expensive process, and as the original data is stored within a CAD system, it seems a natural move to undertake evaluation trials at a virtual level.

Fig. 2.15 shows a simple external view of an attack submarine constructed from approximately 15,000 polygons. Its interior however, is empty, and requires a separate database description that could easily exceed the external complexity by two or three orders of magnitude.

Designers of aero engines also build physical mock ups of their latest designs to ensure that it is physically possible to build them without design faults such as intersecting pipes, inaccessible components, etc. Again, such mockups are very expensive to construct, and as the original design is stored within a CAD system, it seems natural to evaluate the physical requirements of the engine at a virtual level.

The benefits of VEs over physical environments are obvious. No space is required; they can be very accurate and realistic; they can be animated; they can be illuminated; they can be copied, they can be shared; they can be navigated; and one can interact with them. What more could one want?

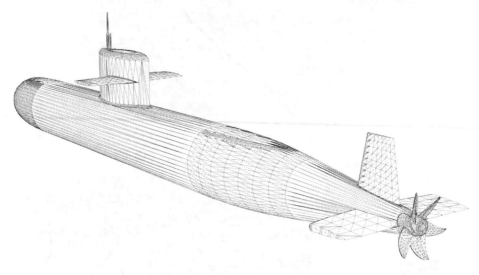

Fig. 2.15 *An attack submarine modeled from 15,000 polygons.*
(Image courtesy of Viewpoint DataLabs)

However, in spite of these obvious advantages, they still require building, which takes time and special modeling software tools. But as we have just seen, they can easily be converted from CAD databases, and processed to support the requirements of a VR system.

Libraries

In the early days of computer animation 3D computer models were often very simple and consisted of logos, words and primitive geometric forms. But with the advent of 3D digitizers and CAD systems more complex models were employed. It was soon realized that such objects had an intrinsic value, and it was futile exercise to model something when the geometry already existed. Perhaps the largest database of 3D geometry is currently held by Viewpoint DataLabs International. Their catalog currently lists over 10,000 3D models covering the sectors of air transport, anatomy, animals, architecture, characters, electronics, geography, ground transport, household, industrial, military, leisure, and space. Everything from a human foot to a Harrier jump-jet is available as a set of polygons or NURBS (Non-Uniform Rational B-Splines, which are a useful type of curve). Fig. 2.16 shows a detailed model of a human head revealing its polygonal structure. Detail such as hair, eyebrows, eyelashes and color must be added separately.

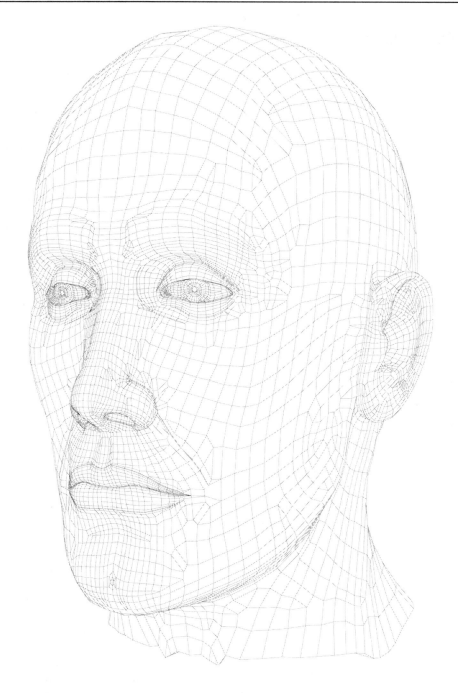

Fig. 2.16 *Polygonal model of a human head.*
(Image courtesy of Viewpoint DataLabs)

Applications

Although I do not want to spend too much time at this stage describing various applications for VR, perhaps it is worth exploring the scope and breadth of applications that are potentially possible.

VR has obvious applications in visualizing structures developed using CAD. The benefits of seeing a product as a true 3D object are immense, and the ability to explore issues of operator visibility, maintenance, manufacture, and physical simulation before anything is built are immeasurable.

VR has significant benefits in training, especially where it is expensive or dangerous to undertake the training using real systems such as planes, ships, power stations, oil rigs, etc.

VR can be used to visualize large building projects where environmental issues are important, and it is important to obtain both exterior and interior views.

VR can be used in surgical training, where a surgeon can practice surgical procedures on virtual organs, without endangering the lives of real patients.

VR can be used in totally original ways, such as for virtual television studios, real-time animated characters for children's programs, and a virtual environment for rehearsing plays.

VR can be used for building virtual museums, virtual historic buildings, and virtual archaeological sites.

And VR can be used for a million-and-one other applications from art to space exploration.

Summary

When VR systems first emerged from university research labs and were offered to industry as a revolutionary design and visualization tool, it was very difficult to convince industry to embrace the technology. There were confused messages about the applications for VR: Apparently VR could be used for computer games, keyhole surgery simulators, education and training, engineering design, scientific visualization, the treatment of phobias, and a million-and-one other applications. But there was little evidence of such applications, and those that did exist were not very convincing.

Since these heady days of hype and promise, industry has had an opportunity of putting VR through its paces and helping in its growth. Various industrial sectors have recognized true potential for VR and have worked with VR companies to design systems they can use. Today, it is not difficult to identify the benefits of virtual reality. The examples we have discussed in this chapter are not contrived, nor are they imaginary—they are all happening today.

It has at last been recognized that it takes time to introduce a revolutionary idea. Real commercial benefits must always be identified and quantifiable, and none of this can be rushed. Industry, technology and commercial climates will dictate the speed with which VR is embraced as an industrial tool.

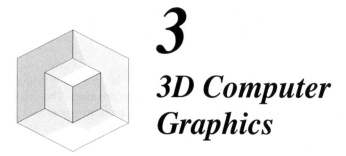

3
3D Computer Graphics

Introduction

As you have probably realized, VR is basically about 3D computer graphics, and in this chapter we are going to explore some of the techniques used to produce colored views of Virtual Environments (VEs).

Computer graphics is an enormous subject, and we only will have time to look at some of the major topics relevant to VR. These include representing 3D VEs, producing a perspective view, and coloring the image. Building the VE is called modeling, whilst image creation is called rendering.

To begin with though, I will put computer graphics in some sort of historical context and show how VR first emerged.

From computer graphics to virtual reality

Computers

In the early 1960s digital computers started to make an impact upon commercial organizations and educational institutes. The machines were very large, often requiring air conditioning and several human operators to load punched cards, paper tape, magnetic tapes, and printer paper. Memory size was measured in kilobytes and a 32KB machine could cost in the order of $100K.

Graph plotters

In the early days, the computer's only graphical peripheral was the graph plotter, that drew lines on paper using a biro or ink pen. The size of these devices varied from a dozen inches to several feet, and the drawing speed could vary from a sluggish 3 cm/sec to 100 cm/sec. Some drawings might only take a few minutes but others could easily exceed an hour, and in spite of these display speeds it was soon realized that computers could be used for animation.

To create an animation sequence a program was designed to draw the individual frames upon animation cells that were then back painted and photographed. It was a tedious process, but even then, the computer was seen as a revolutionary creative tool.

Storage tube displays

In the 1970s the storage tube transformed computer graphics by providing a high-resolution screen for displaying monochrome (green) line drawings. The major disadvantage of the device was that the only way to erase part of the screen was to erase the entire screen. Thus it was useless for any form of moving image. The screen contents could be output to paper using a special thermal printer.

Video displays

Video displays exploited the technology of television to use a video signal to produce an image in the form of colored dots and lines. Video technology however, provided a mechanism for selective erasure, and simple animation.

Frame-stores

As computer memory became cheaper and more abundant, the frame-store emerged in the mid-1970s. This was capable of storing a single image in the form of a matrix of pixels and opened up the possibility of shaded images. It could still take anything from a few minutes to an hour to create a single image that was output to a video disk or video recorder.

Rendering

Shading algorithms appeared in the 1970s notably from Gouraud (Gouraud, 1971) and Phong (Phong, 1973), and texture mapping from James Blinn (Blinn, 1976). Other topics such as anti-aliasing, shadows, hidden-surface removal, environment mapping, and modeling strategies kept researchers busy in the USA and the UK.

Real-time graphics

Towards the end of the 1970s Ivan Sutherland was experimenting with simple real-time image generators that were eventually embraced by the flight simulation industry. By the early 1980s the flight simulator industry became the first to employ VR techniques without realizing it. To them, real-time computer graphics was simulation, and we had to wait a few years for Jaron Larnier to coin the term 'virtual reality'.

Virtual reality

Since 1965 Ivan Sutherland had realized that computers had an important role to play in real-time graphics, and his early work on HMDs was a constant reminder what the future had in store. However, as with many inventions it can take ten to twenty years before an idea is truly realized. Nevertheless, over the past two decades we have witnessed a series of major events that collectively have resulted in today's VR systems. Such events include Cinerama in 1952, Morton Heilig's 'Sensorama' system in 1956, Dan Sandin and Richard Sayre's bend-sensing glove in 1977. The Polhemus tracking system in 1979. Andy Lippman's interactive video disk to drive around Aspen in 1980.

In 1982 Thomas Zimmerman patented a data glove that used optical sensors, and in 1983 Mark Callahan built a see-through HMD at MIT.

During this creative period of invention and discovery various companies pioneered the development of VR hardware and software: notably VPL Research, Inc., W Industries Ltd., Division Ltd., Fakespace, Inc., Polhemus, Virtual Research, Reflection Technologies, Sense 8 Corporation, and Superscape Ltd. Many still exist today, but some, alas, have not managed to survive the intense commercial pressures that pose a constant threat to any embryonic technology.

Modeling objects

Computer graphics techniques are employed to visualize a wide variety of things such as graphs, histograms, business graphics, cars, ships, airplanes, dinosaurs, tornadoes, pigs, water and clouds. To cope with such a wide range of subjects, an equally wide range of tools has evolved to meet the individual requirements of these different structures.

One of the simplest modeling elements used in computer graphics is a flat surface, or polygon. For example, to model a rectangular box, six polygons are required to define its surface (Fig. 3.1). Polygons are ideal for constructing all sorts of regular objects such as bricks, rooms, desks, etc., but are useless for modeling clouds and fog.

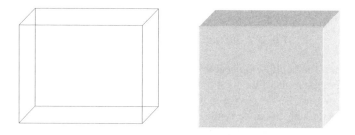

Fig. 3.1 *Wire frame and shaded view of a 6-sided box.*

To appreciate how a 3D object is stored inside a computer, let us examine a simple example. Fig. 3.2 shows an object constructed from 4 triangles: a base, two vertical sides, and the side facing us. The vertices (corners) are labeled *a*, *b*, *c* and *d*. Each triangle can be identified by its vertices: the side facing us is *abc*; the base is *acd*; and the two sides are *cbd* and *adb*. Notice that the vertices are defined in a clockwise sequence as seen from a position outside the object.

The object is stored as a Triangle Table and a Vertex Table. The Triangle Table stores a list of triangles: *abc*, *cbd* and *adb*, and for each triangle there is a list of vertices. For example, triangle *cbd* has vertices *c*, *b* and *d*. With reference to the Vertex Table vertex *c* has coordinates (1, 0, 0); *b* has coordinates (0, 1, 0); and *d* has coordinates (0, 0, 0). The numbers in brackets are the *x*, *y* and *z* coordinates respectively.

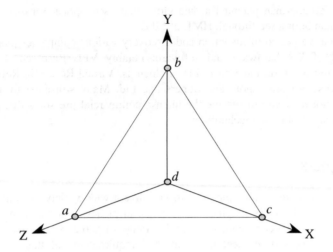

Triangle Table			
name	Vertices		
abc	a	b	c
cbd	c	b	d
adb	a	d	b

Vertex Table			
name	x	y	z
a	0	0	1
b	0	1	0
c	1	0	0
d	0	0	0

Fig. 3.2 *Internal storage of a 3D object.*

The reason for building objects this way is that it is easy to change the geometry of an object. For example, if we wish to move vertex *b* to a new position, all we have to do is alter the Vertex Table with a new set of coordinates. The Triangle Table remains unaltered, as the object's underlying geometry has not changed.

Objects such as teapots, telephones, vases, cars, etc., have complex curved surfaces that can be constructed from curved patches. Fig. 3.3 shows how the delicate curves of a modern telephone can be modeled from a collection of surface patches. Even the coiled cable can be modeled with great accuracy.

Other objects that must incorporate interior detail, as well as their surface geometry, such as engineering components, are constructed using CAD systems, and the techniques are beyond the scope of this text.

Polygons and triangles are very easy to manipulate within a computer and it is possible to create colored views of them extremely fast. Although other modeling techniques can be used to model objects more accurately, the rendering time, in general, is longer.

We will discover that high-speed rendering is vital to a successful VR system. If there is any delay in producing the images seen by the user, the illusion of immersion and presence are quickly lost. Consequently, the majority of VR systems are built around VEs modeled from polygons or triangles. Between the two, triangles are preferred, as they are consistent, i.e. they have 3 sides, and they are always flat. A polygon built from 4 or more sides can be twisted, which can introduce errors in rendering. Fig. 3.4 illustrates how a hexagon would be divided into four triangles.

Fig. 3.3 *A virtual telephone modeled from surface patches.*
(Image courtesy of James Hans)

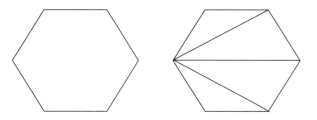

Fig. 3.4 *A single hexagon and a triangulated hexagon.*

Objects in the real world are three-dimensional—that is, three measurements are required to fix the position of a point in space. Similarly, when describing a polygon for

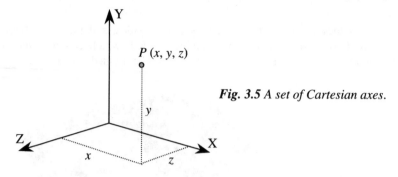

Fig. 3.5 A set of Cartesian axes.

a VE, each vertex (corner) requires three measurements to locate it relative to some reference point called the *origin*. In fact, every polygon in a VE must be described in this way.

Fig. 3.5 shows a set of 3D Cartesian axes (90° to each other) labeled X, Y, and Z, intersecting at the origin. These are used to derive the three measurements (coordinates) for each vertex. In this case the point P has coordinates (x, y, z). Fig. 3.6 shows a triangle that has three vertices, and requires a total of nine coordinates to fix the vertex positions. More complex objects may require hundreds, thousands, or even hundreds of thousands of coordinates, which can present serious computational problems for the VR host computer. It should not be difficult to appreciate that the number of coordinates is proportional to the complexity of the VE, and the larger this size, the longer it takes to render the image. Consequently, every effort is made to keep the VE as simple as possible.

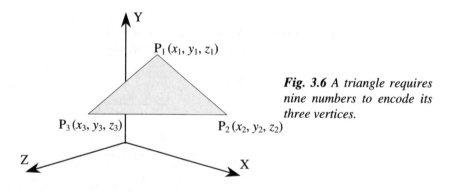

Fig. 3.6 A triangle requires nine numbers to encode its three vertices.

Special 3D modeling systems are available to construct VEs. Systems such as 3D Studio, MultiGen, LightWave, Softimage and Alias/Wavefront, are all used to create the coordinate data. When a CAD system has been used, special programs (filters) can be used to convert the CAD data into a polygonal form acceptable to the VR system. For example, McDonnell Douglas use the Unigraphics II CAD/CAM system to model systems such as the F/A-18 tactical strike fighter engine, but they also use Division's dVISE VR software for visualization purposes. To import such CAD databases

Division provide a range of filters that include Parametric Technologies, Unigraphics II, CADDS5, Pro/ENGINEER, I-DEAS Master Series, CATIA, and Intergraph Solid Edge.

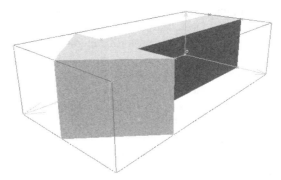

Fig. 3.7 *A 3D arrow created by extruding an outline.*

Certain objects possess different degrees of symmetry. For example, a rectangular box can be imagined as its cross-section extruded over its length, and a cylinder can be imagined as a circle extruded over its height. Fig. 3.7 shows how a 3D arrow can be created from the shape of an arrow. In order to simplify the construction of such objects inside a computer, special modeling tools are available to aid this process.

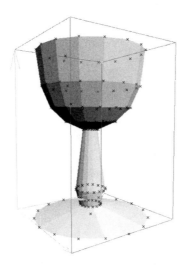

Fig. 3.8 *A wine glass created a sweeping a contour.*

Another class of object exhibit symmetry about an axis. For example, the wine glass shown in Fig. 3.8 has a central vertical axis, about which the glass's contour rotates. This and other objects like cups, saucers, teapots, wheels, etc., can be modeled by first designing a simple contour curve, which is then rotated about an axis to develop the surface. However, when we draw a curve in the real world it is a smooth continuous line—in a computer it has to be represented as a mathematical equation or a string of straight edges. CAD systems employ mathematical techniques, whilst VR systems employ simple strings of straight edges. Thus what should appear to be smooth surfaces are often chunky with an obvious faceted structure. No doubt one day, VR systems will be able to handle perfectly smooth objects, but for the moment, models have to be kept as simple as possible.

Extruding and sweeping techniques can be further developed to construct some really complex objects, which saves considerable time when building a VE.

Although 3D modeling systems permit any object to be built from scratch, they also give the user access to a library of pre-built objects. A simple library facility may only provide a variety of boxes, pyramids, spheres, cylinders, cones, etc., but a more advanced facility may give the user access to hundreds of 3D objects, and perhaps entire VEs. For example, Superscape's DO 3D and VRT systems provide an extensive warehouse of objects that include geometric primitives, buildings, lights, people, plants, streets and toys. Fig. 3.9 shows a typical range of geometric primitives.

Fig. 3.9 *Geometric primitives.*
(Courtesy of James Hans)

Dynamic objects

The whole idea of VR is to allow a user to navigate and interact with a VE. Thus when a user dons a HMD they will be tempted to reach out and touch some of the polygons and move them. This cannot happen unless the VE has been so constructed. For example, if the user wants to move specific vertices then they must be identified within the database during the modeling stage. It would be unusual to allow the user to modify all of the vertices as this could easily destroy the geometric integrity of the VE.

In the case of the user wanting to move an individual polygon or triangle, we must make sure that the polygon's edges are not shared by other polygons. If the edge is shared, then it cannot be moved, because it does not have an independent identity. Fig. 3.10 shows three such polygons that are completely independent of one another.

When the user needs to move an entire object such as a chair, software tools are available to update the VE database with this knowledge. Thus when a user interacts with the VE within an immersive system, their virtual hand can be tested for a collision condition with the object. When a collision occurs, the user can instruct the system for the object to be moved to another position using hand gestures. For non-immersive systems a mouse is used to select an object and move it to a new position.

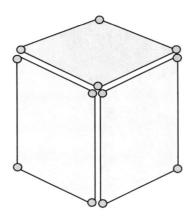

Fig. 3.10 *Three polygons with geometric independence.*

Constraints

Some objects in the VE may require being unconstrained, but others will require constraining in some form or another. For example, the chair shown in Fig. 3.11 could be constrained to rotate about its base, have an adjustable back, move freely across the floor, but prevented from being lifted off the floor. The handset of a virtual telephone, for example, must be unconstrained so that the user can lift it up and manipulate it freely. On the other hand, a door opening into a room requires to be constrained. In real life, a door is constrained by the action of its hinges and the door's frame, which prevent it from rotating indefinitely. If a virtual door is to behave like its real counterpart, it too, must be constrained to rotate through a specified angle.

Imagine a user immersed within a VE and sees a door in front of them. As they approach the door their virtual hand collides with the coordinate geometry of the door.

This is detected by the host computer and allows the user to open the door using appropriate hand gestures. And if the user attempts to open the door beyond its constrained angle, the system simply prevents the action from occurring. If this were not so, it would be mayhem—there would be chairs flying around the room, doors swinging indefinitely about their hinges, and tables imbedded in the walls! Fig. 3.12 shows how a wardrobe would have to be modeled and constrained to allow its doors and draws to be opened.

Fig. 3.11 *A virtual swivel chair.*
(Image courtesy of James Hans)

Fig. 3.12 *A virtual wardrobe showing constraints on doors and draws.*
(Images courtesy of James Hans)

Collision detection

We have already come across the idea of virtual collisions, and perhaps now is a good time to explain how they work. To begin with, imagine a virtual teapot complete with spout, handle and lid. It is probably constructed from 100 triangles, or so. One method of implementing collision detection is to surround the teapot by an invisible box called a 'collision volume', which is stored alongside the teapot's surface geometry in the database. If we lift up the virtual teapot with collision detection activated the teapot can be moved about freely. However, if we bring the teapot too close to another object's collision volume, the host VR computer will detect the coordinates of the collision volumes touching or intersecting. When this occurs, any number of things could happen: to begin with, the intersection is prevented from happening, no matter how the user may force it to happen; the teapot's color could change to indicate a collision has occurred; or the teapot could force the other object to move.

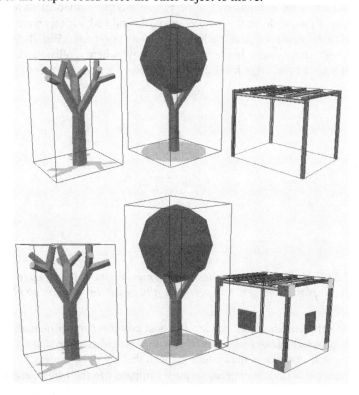

Fig. 3.13 *Non-intersecting and intersecting collision volumes.*
(Images courtesy of Superscape)

Now the idea of being able to move objects around a VE is very important, and the idea of allowing one object to collide with another opens up all sorts of possibilities.

We will return to this matter later in the book—for now, though, let us continue with understanding more about collisions.

If the collision volume of the teapot is nothing more than a box, then we cannot expect a high level of realism when collisions occur. For example, if we slowly move the teapot towards a virtual cup and saucer, at some stage the collision volumes will touch. And if we continue to bring the teapot closer we will see the cup move away, even though the teapot and cup are not touching. Their collision volumes are touching, but not the polygons that make up the teapot and cup. In this trivial example we can cope with this visual error, but in a commercial engineering application it could be vital that the virtual objects must touch, rather than their collision volumes.

Fig. 3.13 shows two trees and a pergola with their collision volumes not intersecting and intersecting. But even when the collision volumes intersect, the enclosed objects are not touching. If greater accuracy is required to detect collisions then a price has to be paid for its implementation. For example, instead of placing a collision volume around the entire object, collision volumes can be placed around individual elements. In the case of the teapot this could be the handle, spout, lid and body. If this were not accurate enough, collision volumes could enclose individual polygons. And if this were not accurate enough, one could implement a strategy where collision detection was performed at a vertex and edge level. Fig. 3.14 shows four ways a pair of triangles can collide.

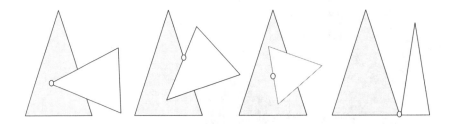

Fig. 3.14 *Four ways two triangles can interact: vertex to plane, edge to edge, edge to plane, and vertex to vertex. A fifth possibility is plane to plane.*

Now these different strategies require the host computer to do increasing levels of work comparing hundreds of thousands of coordinates, and at some stage it will become so great that it will slow down the system so much that it will be useless.

One can see that we are attempting to push computers to their limit, especially PCs. But VR systems have to undertake a lot of work. They have to manipulate large databases of coordinates, support interaction, support collision detection, produce colored pictures, monitor where the user's head and hand are in space, and maintain a real-time performance. If the system becomes 'jerky' because of inadequate processing power, then it can be intolerable. So although we would like high fidelity images and physical realism, it is not always possible, and a compromise has to be struck. For further information on collision detection see Kamat (1993).

Perspective views

Having looked at some of the issues associated with creating a VE using coordinates, let us see how it is possible to develop a perspective view of a VE.

Fortunately, this is very simple and even though the maths is easy I will describe the process visually. If you wish to find out more about this subject, there are plenty of books available that explain how to perform this operation. (Vince, 1995).

To begin with, imagine you are in a room gazing outside through a window. Outside the building you can see trees, houses, roads and clouds. If you wish to draw this view and show different features of the scene in perspective, then the following procedure can be used. First take a marker pen (a white board marker pen is preferable, especially if you wish to erase your masterpiece!) and stand at arm's length in front of the window and gaze straight ahead. Now without moving your head, draw upon the glass the scene outside. You will trace out contours and silhouettes of objects, and those objects further away from you will appear naturally smaller.

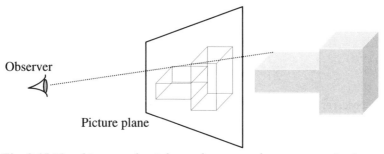

Fig. 3.15 *The objects on the right can be captured as a perspective image on the central picture plane by tracing lines back to the eye on the left.*

What you have drawn is a perspective view of the outside scene, and it would be similar to a photograph captured by a camera. Obviously, the view drawn on the window is influenced by your position in the building: the higher up you are, the more you see the tops of outside objects; the further away you are, the smaller the objects appear.

Now this drawing exercise is very simple to explain, and equally simple to implement within a computer. One simply projects the 3D database of coordinates through an imaginary window called the *picture plane* and convert them to a flat image as shown in Fig. 3.15. To obtain the different viewpoints the projection technique must know where the user's viewpoint is—but in a VR system this is always being monitored for this very purpose. For an immersive system, whenever the user moves their head, it is detected by the VR tracking system, which feeds it back to the computer. The computer, in turn, passes it onto the perspective software program that ensures that the user is always seeing an appropriate view. If there is any lag in the system, whether it be from the 3D tracker, or passing the data within the computer, the user sees images that appear a fraction of a second behind their head movements. This can be extremely distracting.

3D clipping

When you are gazing through the window drawing the perspective scene, you can only see objects in front of you. Walls mask objects behind you and outside of your normal field of view. This masking of unwanted information must be implemented within the computer, otherwise we will be overwhelmed by views of every object within the VE.

The process of removing unwanted detail is called *3D clipping*, and as this is another task for the computer, and is often implemented in hardware for high speed, rather than software. Fig. 3.16 shows the clipping volume in the shape of a pyramid. In this case, only one triangle is completely visible to the observer, the other triangles are only partially visible, as indicated by the shaded areas.

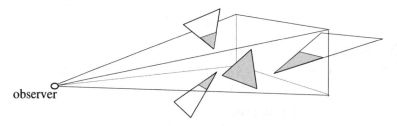

Fig. 3.16 *Only the shaded parts of triangles are visible to the observer.*

Imagine, then, a VR user inside a virtual house. As the user gazes in one direction, objects behind the viewer are being clipped from their view. And if they turn around and face in the opposite direction they will see these objects, whilst the computer removes the previous ones from their view. If the user were now to float vertically through the ceiling towards the first floor, the clipping software will ensure that even when the user's head moves through the ceiling to emerge in a bedroom, all of the polygons are correctly clipped. Thus we can see that clipping is an important process as it enables us to pass miraculously through walls and ceilings without creating any spurious images.

Stereoscopic vision

Most life forms have evolved with pairs of eyes—as two views give an increased field of view and also assist in the perception of depth. You may have experienced the excellent 3D effect that is created when looking at a pair of photographs through a stereoscope. Because the two images are taken from two different positions in space, the brain uses these differences to create a single image that contains depth information. This is called *stereoscopic vision*.

Obviously our own vision system is stereoscopic, and is something we take for granted. We depend upon it to undertake take the more tricky tasks such as threading a needle, sewing, fixing a nut onto a screw, etc.—tasks involving dexterity and precision. But we also depend upon it, but to a lesser extent, to estimate the distance of an approaching car.

Stereoscopic vision is easily created within a VR system—we simply produce two views of the VE, one for the left eye, and the other for the right eye. This means that the perspective software must be given the distance between our eyes, which introduces the first problem. This distance changes from person-to-person, but a typical value of 6.5 cm will suffice. The software can now produce two distinct views of the VE—one 3.25 cm to the left of our gaze, and one 3.25 cm to the right. This increases further the work for the host computer, which now has two images to render!

Because of this extra load for the computer, it is still usual to find monoscopic systems where the left and right eyes see the same image. Naturally, there is no depth information, and the user must learn how to interact without depth cues.

Rendering the image

The next stage is to render the image in the form of pixels so it can be displayed upon a screen or HMD. There are several ways of achieving this: some techniques are very fast and produce an obvious 'computer look'—others take much longer but produce images that look like a real photograph. You can guess which technique is used in VR! It is not that we are deliberately trying to produce simple computer-generated images—we are doing everything in our power to ensure that there is no unwanted lag or latency in the system. An immersive VR system is appalling if the latency extends to 0.25 second, therefore every thousandth of a second is vital. Ideally, one would like a VR system to be able to update the VE 50 times a second (50 Hz, pronounced Hertz), with a latency of no more than 50 ms.

Color

Research has shown that the human eye samples the visible spectrum in three overlapping frequency bands with maximum sensitivities in the red, green and blue colors. These colors have been adopted as the three additive primary colors for mixing light sources, whilst yellow, cyan and magenta are the corresponding subtractive primary colors for mixing paint pigment.

Computer technology uses mixtures of red, green and blue (rgb) to describe color and it is convenient to specify a color as three numbers that range from 0 to 1. Thus an rgb triplet of (0, 0, 0) represents black, and (1, 1, 1) represents white. Table 3.1 shows other values for rgb triplets and the corresponding color, and Fig. 3.17 provides a spatial way of interpreting this RGB data.

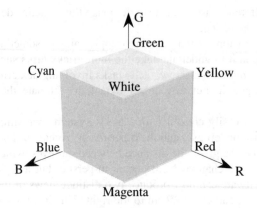

Fig. 3.17 *The RGB color space.*

Although a color can be represented as an rgb triplet it is not very intuitive, and it is difficult to search for a specific color simply by adding or subtracting different amounts of red, green and blue. In an attempt to resolve this problem the HSVcolor space is also used to represent the quantities hue, saturation and value. To begin with, a number between 0 and 1 determines a particular hue; then saturation, which also varies between 0 and 1, controls the amount of white light in the color; and finally, value represents the brightness of the mixed color.

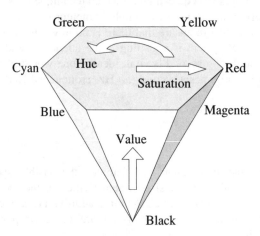

Fig. 3.18 *The HSV color space.*

Fig. 3.18 illustrates the HSV color space, and as both systems have their respective strengths, they are both used in user interfaces to describe color.

Table 3.1 *Values of red, green and blue and the resulting color*

Red	Green	Blue	Color
0	0	0	Black
0	0	1	Blue
0	1	0	Green
0	1	1	Cyan
1	0	0	Red
1	0	1	Magenta
1	1	0	Yellow
1	1	1	White

Colored objects

After an object is modeled it is assigned a color. This may be selected from a given palette of colors or a particular mix of the video primary colors: red, green and blue. The entire model may have one color, or it may be that different sides or polygons have specific colors—virtually anything is possible.

You will probably know that a television screen is constructed from a matrix of discrete picture elements called *pixels*, and each pixel has a red, green and blue phosphor dot. When three electron beams scan these pixels, the phosphors glow according to the intensity of the beams. This Cathode Ray Technology (CRT) is only found in high-quality HMDs, and for every-day HMDs liquid crystal display (LCD) technology is used: it is lighter, cheaper, smaller and readily available. Whether the display technology is CRT, LCD or video projectors, the images are represented as a matrix of pixels.

Before an image is displayed it is formed inside the computer's memory by the renderer program. Whilst this process is underway, the previous image is being displayed. This overlapping of computer tasks is another method of keeping the VR system running as fast as possible.

The renderer uses the perspective view of an object to determine which pixels have to be updated, and the color of the object is used to flood the relevant pixels. The image can be made to look life-like by coloring the object with color shades that give the impression it is lit by some light source. Another way is to let the renderer automatically work out the surface shading of the object. To do this, the renderer is given the position and intensity of a virtual light source, and using some simple laws of illumination, shades the object with acceptable color intensities.

Shading algorithms range from the very simple to the very complex: Gouraud shading is found in most VR systems and renders polygons with subtle changes of intensity and color over a polygon. The resultant image produces a matte effect, but is acceptable for most applications. Where it is important to see reflections of the illuminating light source Phong shading is used. This takes a little more time to compute but creates more realistic images, especially when the objects are supposed to be reflective. Plates 3 and 4 show two excellent examples of 3D modeling and rendering.

Light sources

To add that extra degree of realism, a variety of light sources can be used to illuminate a VE. These include ambient, spot, fixed point, and parallel. Ambient light is a fixed background light level that has no direction—only color and intensity. It is included in the lighting calculations as a constant term and can account for approximately 25% of the total illumination level. A virtual spotlight simulates the action of its real-world counterpart and has position, direction, spot angle, color and intensity. A fixed point light source is a point in space that radiates light in all directions, and a parallel light source shines light in one direction as though it were located at some distant position like the sun. Together, these sources of light create realistic levels of illumination, but nowhere near as accurate as the radiosity technique.

Lights can be moved about the VE, and even attached to the user's hand to simulate a torch. And as long as the software system provides the facility, any parameter associated with a light can be altered.

Because lights are represented as numerical quantities within a VR system, numbers can be positive and negative. A positive level of intensity represents a normal light source, but a negative value creates a source of darkness. Now this has no equal in the real world, but can be a useful feature.

Rendering algorithms

All renderers are faced with the problem of forming a picture in the frame-store such that objects mask one another correctly. In the field of computer graphics this is known as hidden surface removal. A number of algorithms (techniques) have been developed over the years such as Z-buffering, the scan-line algorithm, painter's algorithm, ray tracing, the A-buffer, etc., and they all have strengths and weaknesses. In VR we are particularly interested in speed—for if it can not run in real time, then it is of little use. I will describe the underlying principles of three of the above algorithms.

Painter's algorithm

As the name suggests, this technique is similar to the way a painter creates a painting. For example, one would start painting the most distant elements such as the sky and horizon line, and over-paint these with objects that are closer to the artist. To implement this in software requires that we know how far each object is away from the viewer. This in itself is not too difficult, but in a VR system the user is continually moving about, and changes his/her relative position to every object. Therefore, it means that for every image, the software has to compute the distance of each object from the viewer; sort the distances in ascending sequence; and render the most distant one first, and the nearest last. This is the basic technique. What we now need are ways of speeding up the process to maximize the renderer's update rate.

A technique used by Superscape is to associate a bounding cube with every object. Although this exists in the database, it is never rendered, unless required for editing purposes. Superscape's VRT system sorts the bounding cubes into distance sequence, and starts by rendering the object whose bounding cube is furthest from the observer, and proceeds with closer and closer objects. For most situations the algorithm works very well, but as it is possible to enclose highly irregular objects by a simple cube, the algorithm is not 100% accurate. However, when such conflicts arise, a Z-buffer algorithm can be used to resolve the situation very effectively.

Scan-line algorithm

A video image is transmitted and displayed on a television screen in the form of horizontal rasters or scan-lines, which is where the scan-line algorithm gets its name. The scan-line algorithm renders the image raster by raster, normally starting at the top, and working its way down to the bottom of the image.

To visualize what is happening, imagine gazing at a scene through a slit as shown in Fig. 3.19 that is as wide as the image but vertically very thin. The algorithm first identifies the objects visible in the slit and proceeds to sort them in distance sequence and loads the raster of colors into the frame store. It then proceeds to the next raster down. But as this is so close to the scan-line above, there is a very good chance that the same objects are visible, and therefore the distance relationships are the same. If an another object comes into view, very little work is needed to adjust for its presence.

This algorithm has also been mixed with other techniques such as the Z-buffer, to create various hybrid renderers.

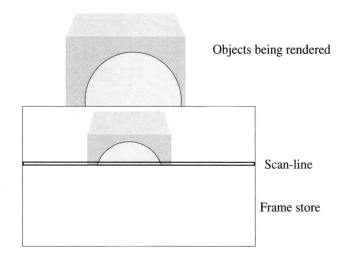

Fig. 3.19 Rendering an image using the scan-line algorithm.

Z-buffer

The *Z-buffer*, or *depth buffer* algorithm, avoids any kind of sorting by memorizing the depth of rendered polygons at a pixel level. Which means that if there are 640 x 480 pixels in the image, there is a corresponding piece of computer memory called the Z-buffer, to record the depth of the polygon covering each pixel. The letter Z is chosen, as it is the Z-axis that points away from the observer when the depth calculations are made.

To visualize how this works, imagine that the Z-buffer is primed with very large depth values, such as 10,000. Say the first polygon to be rendered is 500 units away, every pixel it covers will be rendered and the corresponding positions in the Z-buffer updated with the value 500. If the next polygon to be rendered is 1,000 units away and is masked by the first polygon, the Z-buffer can be used to resolve the masking. For example, if the Z-buffer contains a depth value greater than 1,000 then the new polygon is visible. If, on the other hand, it contains a depth value less than 1,000, it means that a polygon has already been rendered that is closer. Fig. 3.20 shows two views of portions of the Z-buffer. The left view shows the status of the buffer after the first polygon is rendered, and the right view shows the buffer after the second polygon is rendered.

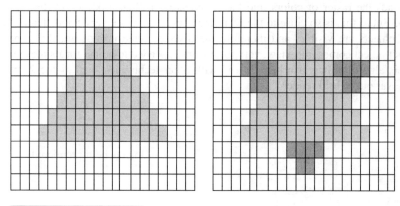

	Depth of 10,000
	Depth of 500
	Depth of 1,000

Fig. 3.20 The two images show how the z-buffer records the depths of the two polygons.

Because depth is maintained at a pixel level the Z-buffer can resolve interpenetrating objects. For example, if a small box intersected a larger sphere, the curves of intersection are revealed automatically by the Z-buffer, which saves an immense amount of modeling time.

Although the Z-buffer is effective at hidden surface removal, the basic algorithm cannot cope with transparency and anti-aliasing. But the latter can be implemented approximately if the Z-buffer stores depths at sub-pixel level.

Texture mapping

If further realism is required, such as reflections, shadows, and spotlights, more advanced techniques are required, which in turn require powerful computers. However, one quick way of incorporating extra realism is with the aid of texture maps. These can be from photographs scanned into the computer or created by paint programs. For example, to make a virtual bookcase look more realistic, a photograph of wood grain can be scanned in and mapped onto the polygons by the renderer. Matching the scale of the texture to the size of the bookcase is important, and if the texture map is insufficient to cover a polygon, it can be repeated like a tile to ensure coverage. Fig. 3.21 shows a wire frame and textured view of a bookcase.

Fig. 3.21 *A wire frame and textured virtual bookcase.*
(Images courtesy of James Hans)

Fig. 3.22 shows a texture from Superscape's DO 3D program, and the effect when it is mapped onto a box.

Mapping texture on objects that remain close the observer is a very effective way of introducing extra detail, but problems arise when the object moves farther away. For example, if the object's size reduces by a factor of 5, the original texture is far too detailed. And if the size reduces by a factor of 10, another level of texture detail is required. This problem was appreciated by Lance Williams (1983) who proposed that a set of texture maps could be used to decorate objects at different distances. The name

MIP mapping or *MIP textures* is given to this strategy. MIP textures also minimize aliasing artifacts that arise when *texels* (texture pixels) are mapped onto screen pixels.

Fig. 3.22 *Planar texture map and its mapping onto a box.*

Billboard textures

When a texture map is used as a backdrop to a scene, such as the one shown in Fig. 3.22, it is called a *billboard texture*. This technique is also used to introduce trees into a scene. A single vertical polygon is placed in a scene, onto which is mapped a photograph of a tree. The trees in Fig. 3.23 are all billboard textures. If we moved around such a tree, we would not discover any depth to the texture, because it is nothing more than a photograph. In image generators, the viewer never sees a side view of the tree, because the tree's polygon is automatically rotated to face the viewer. One would expect that such a trick would be easy to detect, but when the viewer is engaged in some training task, it is unnoticed.

Fig. 3.23 *Real-time textured scene. (Image courtesy of Evans & Sutherland Computer Corporation, Salt Lake City, Utah, USA)*

Dynamic textures

Dynamic textures are a sequence of texture maps applied to a surface in quick succession, and are used to simulate special effects such as flames, explosions, and smoke trails.

Bump mapping

Another way of increasing image realism is *bump mapping* and was developed by Jim Blinn (1978). Basically, it consists of using a texture map to modulate the way light is reflected pixel by pixel. One would normally use photographs of bumpy materials such as concrete, leather, orange peel, etc. lit obliquely. Real-time image generators use the technique to create sea states, as shown in Fig. 3.24.

Fig. 3.24 *Real-time bump mapping. (Image courtesy of Evans &*
Sutherland Computer Corporation, Salt Lake City, Utah, USA)

Environment mapping

Environment mapping simulates the effect of polished surfaces that reflect their surroundings. To a certain extent, it is similar to texture mapping, but an environment map is not fixed to the object's surface—it moves whenever the object moves to create the impression of a reflection. It is particularly useful in the display of car bodies, and shows how reflective highlights travel of the surface of a moving car.

Shadows

Shadows in the real world just happen, but virtual shadows require considerable levels of computation. This is rather unfortunate because shadows do play an important role in the way we interpret the position and orientation of objects in the real world.

Various techniques have been developed to compute shadows, and they all require a geometric analysis of the spatial relationship between light sources and the objects in a scene. Ray tracing is particularly good at creating shadows, so too is radiosity, but neither can be used in real time. However, when a high performance graphics computer is available, it is possible to compute shadows for some scenes in real time.

Because shadows are so important, simple techniques have been developed to introduce some form of a shadow, even though the end result is not perfect. One such technique used in flight simulators and certain computer games consists of sliding a shadow polygon over the ground in synchronization with the motion of an object. A static shadow polygon is shown in Fig. 6.4, and is incorporated as part of the table's geometry. Plates 3, 4, 5 and 6 show how effective computer generated shadows can be.

Radiosity

There are two rendering techniques that create photo-realistic images: ray tracing and radiosity. Ray tracing is excellent for realizing shadows, reflections, refraction, etc., but is far too slow for VR systems. Having said that, currently we are waiting for a new ray tracing processor to appear, which will hopefully transform ray tracing rendering speed. So perhaps one-day computers will become fast enough to support such a technique. Radiosity is an equally slow technique and produces wonderful views of interiors as shown in Fig. 3.25. It achieves this by simulating the internal reflections that arise when an interior is illuminated by light sources. These are represented as a series of simultaneous equations that are solved to find a common solution, which can take anything from a few seconds, minutes or hours—much depends upon the complexity of the model.

Progressive refinement is another way of solving the radiosity model. It begins by looking at the brightest source of light and distributes its energy throughout the model. It then selects the next brightest source and continues to repeat the algorithm until changes in the image are too small to notice.

If the technique takes so long, why are we looking at it if there's no chance of it running in real time? Radiosity is relevant to VR for the following reason: once the algorithm has been used to compute the delicate shades and shadows within a VE, the color intensities can be stored and associated with the individual polygons. From then on, there is no need for any virtual light source—the light intensities and shadows have been 'frozen' onto the polygons, and it is possible to move about the VE in real time. However, if we move an object in the VE it takes with it the original shading, and leaves behind shadows that may have been cast upon a floor or wall. For many applications, especially those where VR is being used for visualization purposes, this is a small price to pay for excellent image quality.

Plates 5 and 6 show two beautiful scenes rendered using the LightWorks rendering system. Plate 5 incorporates reflections that have been calculated using ray tracing—these would not be used if the model were to be used in a VR system, because they are viewer dependent.

Fig. 3.25 *Radiosity interior of a car. (Image courtesy of LightWork Design.*
Produced using the LightWorks rendering system)

Fog

Fog or haze has been used in flight simulator Image Generators (IG) for many years. A simple solution is to fade the color of objects at a certain distance into a gray to give the impression of a background haze. But modern IGs can simulate fog very realistically and simulate the effect of ground fog settling in valleys. Fig. 3.26 shows a real-time image from and Evans & Sutherland IG.

Transparency

Although most objects are opaque, it is essential to be able to simulate transparent materials such as glass, water and certain plastics. Although this can be done, it does have an impact upon the renderer. The Z-buffer technique, for example, renders objects in an arbitrary sequence. And if a transparent object is rendered first, followed by an opaque object, once the transparent object is completed, no information remains to compute how much of the opaque object will be visible. Other types of renderer require access to all of the objects—transparent and opaque—in order that transparency calculations can be made. In VR systems, one has the opportunity of declaring that an object is colored with a certain degree of transparency.

Fig. 3.26 *Real-time image of realistic fog. (Image courtesy of Evans & Sutherland Computer Corporation, Salt Lake City, Utah, USA)*

Because light travels slower in materials such as glass and water, its direction changes and gives rise to refraction. It is possible to calculate such phenomena using ray tracing, but this, at the moment cannot be achieved in real time.

Other computer graphics techniques

Computer graphics consists of many more techniques that will eventually become part of VR. Some of the relevant ones include soft objects, particle systems, NURBS, depth of field, and volumetric rendering.

Soft objects

The majority of objects used in computer graphics are modeled as a boundary skin, and the technique is called *boundary representation* or *B-Rep*. This boundary normally has a polygonal form and is based upon measurements for some physical object. It is also possible to express 3D shapes mathematically. For example, the equation of a sphere reminds us that $radius^2 = x^2 + y^2 + z^2$, where the point (x, y, z) is any point on the sphere's surface. Thus for a given radius, it is possible to find a range of values for x, y and z that satisfy this equation. The next problem is connecting these points into a polygonal boundary representation. The interesting thing is that if equations can be used to model shapes then it's possible to utilize a wide range of mathematical surfaces. For example, we could use the equations used for describing electric and magnetic fields; we could even use equations that described the surface geometry of a drop of water. Such objects are called *soft objects*, because the objects are very rarely rigid. Fig. 3.9 shows a variety of 3D primitives, but in the foreground is a soft object formed from two close spheres. Using this technique it is possible to animate two individual spheres colliding with one another and creating one larger sphere.

Particle systems

Particle systems are used to model large number of points that can be animated to simulate droplets of water, fire, explosions, clouds, and other natural phenomena. They have been used for some time in flight simulators to simulate snow, and they can be animated to reproduce the same visual effect when driving through a snowstorm using landing lights. Each particle is given a position in space, color and lifetime, and by changing these parameters it is possible to reproduce a wide variety of effects that could not be achieved using polygons.

NURBs

A *NURB* or *Non-Uniform Rational B-spline* is a mathematical curve widely used in CAD to describe complex surfaces such as those found on car bodies. They are a very powerful modeling tool and enable a designer to describe a surface in terms of a few curves that can be blended to form a smooth continuous surface. A NURB is created using a set of control points, and as the control points are adjusted the NURB responds by forming a new smooth curve.

Depth of field

The majority of computer-generated images have an infinite depth of field, where every object in the scene is in perfect focus. In reality we know that this does not happen due to the optical structure of the human eye. As we have become accustomed to focusing on an object and noticing that the foreground and background are out of focus, it would be useful to simulate this effect. Using ray tracing, it is possible to introduce depth of field in computer images, but unfortunately not in real time.

Volumetric rendering

The shading techniques such as Gouraud and Phong shading are very simple shaders and only approximate to what happens in reality. Ray tracing and radiosity are much more accurate techniques, but require substantially more time to render a scene. Volumetric rendering simulates another type of natural phenomena that occurs when light intersects a volume of space containing dust, smoke or mist. The technique is very effective and makes computer-generated images much more believable.

Summary

We have seen that computer graphics consists of a variety of techniques concerned with modeling 3D objects and VEs, assigning physical attributes, obtaining a perspective view, and coloring the image. These are standard techniques that have been used in computer animation and CAD for many years. However, these and other applications have never had to work in real time—users have been prepared to wait for anything from a few seconds to a couple of hours for a single image. VR has no choice but to work in real time and this means that ultra fast, computer graphics techniques have to be found to keep latency to a minimum. It is easy to understand why it is difficult to run such techniques in real time, for if we are attempting to update a VE at 25 Hz, there is only 40 ms to create each image, which is very small, even in the time span of a computer.

Unfortunately, there has not been space to go any deeper into these techniques, however, what has been covered is sufficient to understand the role of computer graphics in VR.

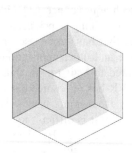

4
Human Factors

Introduction

Before proceeding with the technology of VR it will useful to explore aspects of our selves that will be influenced by this technology—this area is known as *human factors* and covers a wide range of complex topics.

Human factors covers much more than the physical aspects addressed in this chapter. It embraces issues such as:

- Human learning in VEs.
- Spatial cognition, spatial memory, spatial ability in VEs.
- Individual differences in VEs
- Cognitive models for VEs
- Multi-user VE design methods.
- Social interaction within VEs.

These topics, unfortunately, are beyond the scope of this text as researchers around the world are still addressing them, so I will just look at our senses.

The senses for vision, hearing, smell, taste and equilibrium are the normal *special senses*; whereas the senses for tactile, position, heat, cold, and pain are the *somatic senses*. In this chapter however, we will look only at some relevant facts related to the sensory systems exploited by VR technologies. These include vision, hearing, tactile and equilibrium.

Readers who wish to discover more about this interesting subject are recommended to refer to Guyton's *Textbook of Medical Physiology* (Guyton, 1991).

Vision

It is obvious that our visual system is an essential human factor to be taken into account when designing VR hardware and software. The eye and the mechanism of vision is complex, and we have still a long way to go in understanding how the eye and brain work together, not to mention the act of seeing. Fortunately we do not need to know too much about how the eye functions—just enough to understand how it can be best exploited without being abused.

The eye

The eye is a sphere enclosing a lens that focuses light upon the light-sensitive retina fixed to the back of the eyeball. From the retina, signals are processed and transported via the optic nerve to the visual cortex where the action of seeing is organized. Light first enters the eye through the transparent *cornea*, and then through a hole called the *pupil* before being refracted by the lens to focus upon the retina. See Fig. 4.1. But because light is coming from objects at incredible distances such as the moon (400,000

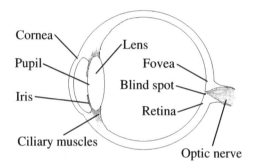

Fig. 4.1 *The human eye.*

km) and from hand-held objects only a few centimeters away, the lens must be able to automatically adjust its refractive power to keep images in focus. This is called *accommodation* and is achieved by contracting and relaxing the ciliary muscles surrounding the lens.

Color receptors

The retina contains two types of light-sensitive cells called *rods* and *cones*. The rods are sensitive to low levels of illumination and are active in night vision; however, they do not contribute towards our sense of color—this is left to the cone cells that are sensitive to three overlapping regions of the visible spectrum: red, green and blue. Collectively, they sample the incoming light frequencies and intensities, and give rise to nerve impulses that eventually end up in the form of a colored image.

The *fovea* is the center of the retina and is responsible for capturing fine colored detail—the surrounding area is still sensitive to color but at a reduced spatial resolution. The fovea enables us to perform tasks such as reading, and if we attempt to read outside of this area, the image is too blurred to resolve any useful detail. The fovea is only 0.1 mm in diameter, which corresponds to approximately 1° of the eye's field of view (FOV). Towards the edge of the retina the cells become very sensitive to changes in light intensity, and provide peripheral vision for sensing movement.

Visual acuity

Acuity is a measure of the eye's resolving power, and because the density of cells varies across the retina, measurements are made at the fovea. An average eye can resolve two bright points of light separated 1.5 mm at a distance of 10 m. This corresponds to 40 seconds or arc, and is equivalent to a distance of 2 microns on the retina.

The blind spot

The brain is connected to each eye via an optic nerve that enters through the back of the eye to connect to the retina. At the point of entry the distribution of rods and cones is sufficiently disturbed to create an area of blindness called the *blind spot*, but this does not seem to cause us any problems. The blind spot is easily identified by a simple experiment. To begin with, close one eye—for example the right eye—then gaze at some distant object with the left eye. Now hold up your left-hand index finger at arm's length slightly left of your gaze direction. Whilst still looking ahead, move your index finger about slowly. You will see the finger tip vanish as it passes over the blind spot. What is strange, is that although the image of the finger disappears, the background in formation remains! It is just as well that this does not create problems for us in the design of HMDs.

Stereoscopic vision

If we move towards an object, the ciliary muscles adjust the shape of the lens to accommodate the incoming light waves to maintain an in-focus image. Also, the eyes automatically converge to ensure that the refracted images fall upon similar areas of the two retinas. This process of mapping an image into corresponding positions upon the two retinas is the basis of *stereoscopic vision*. The difference between the retinal images is called *binocular disparity* and is used to estimate depth, and ultimately gives rise to the sense of 3D. See Fig. 4.2.

Stereopsis cues

In 1832 Charles Wheatstone showed that a 3D effect could be produced by viewing two 2D images using his stereoscope. Brewster went on to perfect the device using prisms instead of the mirrors used by Wheatsone. The 3D image formed by two separate views, especially those provided by the eyes, enable us to estimate the depth of objects, and such cues are called *stereopsis cues*.

It had been assumed that stereoscopic perception was linked to our knowledge of an object, but in 1971 Bela Julesz (1971) showed that it was in fact independent. By viewing patterns of random dots in a stereoscope Julesz was able to show that when the patterns where displaced horizontally, the brain used the image disparity to create three-dimensional depth. The fact that the dot patterns were random showed that the brain did not require knowledge of the image to perceive a 3D effect. Since then random dot stereograms have been available commercially, and although they only consist of a single poster, when viewed carefully, a 3D effect is seen.

A HMD is nothing more than a stereoscope, but instead of photographs animated video images are used. What is essential though, is that the views seen by the two eyes must overlap—and it is in this area of overlap that stereoscopic vision is perceived. Fig. 4.2 shows this diagrammatically, and because the illustrated cube is closer than the cylinder, its image disparity is greater.

Motion parallax cues

Although stereopsis is a very efficient strategy for estimating the depth of objects, the brain has learned that it's always best to have an alternative strategy. In this case, *motion parallax cues* are also used to estimate the depth of moving objects, and uses image speed across the retina as a cue. Furthermore, where stereopsis uses both eyes to compute the disparity between the two views of an object, motion parallax only requires one eye. An object close to the eye will appear to sweep out a large angle across the retina, whereas a distant object will not only be smaller, but it will move through a smaller angle.

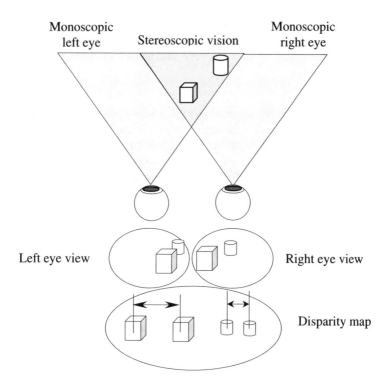

Fig. 4.2 *Diagrammatic description of stereopsis.*

Perspective depth cues

Perspective depth cues arise when we are familiar with the normal size of an object. For example, when we see a large plane such as a Boeing 767 flying, its small size confirms that it is a considerable distance away—for we know that on the ground its size is overwhelming.

The brain does not rely upon one strategy to determine an object's depth—whatever cues are available, whether in the form of motion parallax cues, stereopsis cues, or perspective cues—they all contribute towards a collective answer.

Binocular visual field

Our two eyes produce two overlapping fields of view that create a binocular visual field of approximately ±90° horizontally and ±60° vertically. The area of overlap is about 120°, where stereopsis occurs. For example, if we gaze ahead we are aware that our central field of view is rich in color, and objects are located precisely in space. However, if we fixate upon some central feature of the scene, it is very difficult to distinguish the form of objects positioned at the limit of our peripheral vision. There is no depth sensation, limited color information, but moving objects are easily perceived.

Looking at the world through one eye is still interesting, but one cannot deny the sense of presence that arises when we open the other eye. Stereoscopic vision provides that overwhelming sense of being part of the world that a single eye can never provide. And it is this sense of presence that VR is attempting to mimic through stereoscopic HMDs. However, creating a realistic, wide-angle, binocular visual field is a real technical challenge, which is why CAVES and panoramic screens are becoming so popular.

Image processing

The eye is not just an organic camera—and the way we perceive the world is not just a question of optics. We are endowed with very sophisticated image processing facilities to recognize human faces, the depth of objects, and whether something is upside down or not. For example, because the sun is always above the ground, objects tend to be illuminated at the top, and in shadow at the bottom. Our visual system has adapted to this natural phenomenon and uses it to extract information about the orientation of objects.

Persistence of vision

When we accidentally look at a bright light, an after image can stay with us for some seconds. This is because the retina becomes saturated and requires time to restore the normal levels of chemicals. Apart from this electrochemical latency, our short-term visual memory can hold onto an image long after we close our eyes. This *persistence of vision* enables a series of discrete images repeated at a certain speed to be perceived as continuous. This is called the *Critical Fusion Frequency* (CFF) and depends upon the image brightness, and is around 20 Hz.

Flicker

Persistence of vision is exploited by television and computer displays by refreshing the screen many times a second. The refresh field rate for television is 50 Hz for the UK and 60 Hz for the USA, but some manufacturers have doubled these rates to reduce flicker even further. Flicker can be very tiresome, and in some cases can seriously interfere with the actions of our brain. For example, driving along a tree-lined road with a low sun can be highly dangerous, as the strobing of light and dark can induce an epileptic fit in some people. Indeed, recently in Japan, dozens of children were admitted to hospital after watching a television cartoon containing a sequence of bright flickering images.

Vision and display technology

From this brief description we see that our eyes are constantly working to ensure that we capture anything that could be useful to our survival. However, it is not too difficult to appreciate that our eyes have to behave differently when we don a HMD. To begin with, they are unable to focus upon different objects within the VE—for all objects are in clear focus and light rays all come from the same distance. There are optical distortions that in no way contribute towards creating a sense of presence, and there are physiological problems that arise from conflicts in accommodation and convergence.

Optical distortions

The optical distortions found in HMDs arise from the optical elements used to collimate the image. Such distortions include *astigmatism*, *barrel* and *pincushion distortion*, *chromatic* and *spherical aberration*. Non-spherical lenses introduce a double image when a point is viewed off axis—this is called astigmatism. Barrel and pincushion distortion are when the optical system becomes non-linear either horizontally or vertically, and their effects are shown in Fig. 4.3. Chromatic aberration is when light of

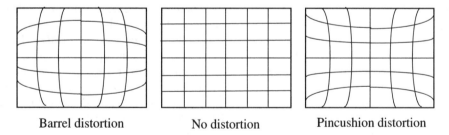

Barrel distortion   No distortion   Pincushion distortion

***Fig. 4.3** Barrel and pincushion distortion.*

different wavelengths focuses at different points, and is removed by an achromatic lens combination. And spherical aberration is due to changes in focal length across the diameter of a lens.

Collimation distance

The lens combination placed in front of the LCD or the CRT units determines the distance at which the image appears to be located, and is known as the *collimation distance*. In certain flight simulator displays the collimation distance approximates to infinity. In fact, this is a theoretical value—in practice it varies between several hundred meters to several thousand meters. Either way, the images appear to be located at a great distance.

In real life, light waves traveling from a distant mountain have a large radius of curvature when they arrive at our eyes. Whereas, the radius of curvature of light waves emanating from a nearby object is considerably smaller. It is this difference in curvature that requires the eye's lens to change shape if near and far objects are to be seen in focus. Now if we look into a display system collimated to infinity, our eyes will relax to accommodate the image. And because the light appears to come from infinity, there is a natural expectation for the image content to contain appropriate objects associated with a distant landscape. If however, we attempt to display an object that should appear relatively close, there is an immediate conflict. The motion parallax cues are wrong; eye convergence is minimal; and our ciliary muscles are relaxed. The overall sensation is very strange and still causes some problems for the flight simulation industry.

The reverse can be found in HMDs. If these are collimated to two or three meters say, it is difficult to display distant objects with any realism. However, given a little time, we can adapt to these anomalies.

Depth of field

In the real world, we perceive objects located at different distances, because the light waves reaching our eyes have different radii of curvature. Within a certain tolerance there is a depth of field that is in focus—objects that are before or beyond this zone are out of focus. This is a useful feature of our visual system as it permits us to concentrate upon specific objects without being distracted by unwanted information.

Currently, display technology cannot collimate at a pixel level—the entire image is collimated at one distance; and although it is possible to adjust to this effect it is not an ideal solution. It is fortuitous that the Z-buffer rendering technique employs a depth buffer to store the depth detail for every pixel. Hopefully, one day, it will be possible to exploit this information to develop a HMD with a true depth of field.

One of the biggest disappointments of early VR systems was the HMDs. Their resolution was so poor that individual pixels were visible, and the optical sensation was similar to looking through two cardboard tubes! Attempting to create a real sensation of presence within the VE was very difficult, as one was constantly aware of the imperfections of the HMD. Today, although very high quality display devices exist that provide excellent resolution (see Appendix B), a HMD does not exist that in any way matches the technical specification of our own visual system.

Hearing

Sound, like color, is a creation of the brain. Pressure waves that impinge upon our ears give rise to an amazing spectrum of auditory sensations that provide a medium for speech and music, not to mention the everyday noises from trains, cars, telephones, and alarm bells.

The ear

For our purposes it is convenient to divide the ear into three parts: the *outer ear, middle ear* and the *inner ear*. The outer ear consists of the *pinna*, which we normally call the ear. It has quite a detailed shape and plays an important role in capturing sound waves, but more importantly, it shapes the spectral envelope of incident sound waves. This characteristic will be explored further when we examine sound direction.

The middle ear consists of the *tympanic membrane* (the eardrum) and the *ossicular system*, which conducts sound vibrations to the inner ear via a system of interconnecting bones. The *cochlea* is located in the inner ear, and is responsible for discriminating loudness and frequency. Finally, signals from the cochlea are interpreted by the brain's auditory cortex as the sensation of sound.

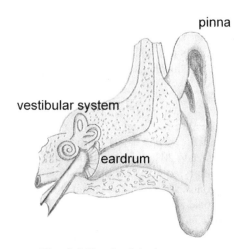

Fig. 4.4 Sketch of the human ear.

Speed, frequency, wavelength and volume

Sound waves travel through any solid, gas or liquid, and for each medium there is a speed of propagation. In air the speed is approximately 344 m/s, which is very slow compared to the speed of light—300,000 km/s! Where different frequencies of light give rise to sensations of color, different frequencies of sound are detected as changes in pitch. It is the subtle mixture of frequencies that make up the different sounds we associate with objects such as a piano, violin, drum or a wine glass being hit by a spoon.

A young person's frequency range extends approximately from 20 to 20,000 cycles per second, but as we age, this can reduce to 50 to 8,000 cycles per second. If one visualizes a sound wave as a cyclic disturbance of air molecules moving forwards and backwards, the wavelength of the sound wave is the distance between two corresponding points in successive cycles, and is different for different frequencies. See Fig. 4.5. For example, at a frequency of 20 c/s, the wavelength is 17.2 m; and at 20,000 c/s the wavelength reduces to 17.2 mm. However, these distances are not fixed, because the velocity of sound in air depends upon its temperature.

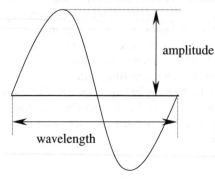

Fig. 4.5 Amplitude and wavelength of a waveform.

The amplitude of the pressure waves controls the sound volume, and the ear is particularly adept in detecting the faintest whisper to the most intense explosion. This range of sound intensities results in oscillations in the inner ear with an amplitude ratio of 1 to 1 million. However, this difference in sound level eventually gets compressed to a 10,000-fold change.

Direction

When a door bangs shut, pressure waves spread through the air and eventually impinge upon our ears. Perhaps the left ear may detect the pressure waves before the right ear, and as our ears are approximately 20 cm apart, a time delay of 0.6 ms arises, that can be detected by the brain's auditory cortex. This obviously is something the brain uses to assist in locating the horizontal source of the sound, but it does not explain how we locate the source in the vertical plane. The interaction of the sound wave with our head and the pinnae play a significant role in shaping its spectral content.

Sounds from different directions are influenced differently by the geometry of our head and ears, and our brains are able to exploit this interaction to localize the sound source. This is easily demonstrated by 'cupping' one's hands and placing them close to one's ears—ambient sounds are immediately 'colored'. If our 'cupped' hands have this affect upon sounds, it is only natural that our ears must modify the spectral characteristics before the waves travel towards the inner ear. Research by Shaw (1974) confirmed this phenomenon, and showed that the spectral shaping was dependent upon the spatial origin of the sound source.

Sound stage

When we look at the real world we are convinced that what we see is physically independent of us and that we are a natural part of it. For example, as I look through my office window I can see trees and houses and I like to believe that what I see is out there. But we know that this is not true—what we see is experienced *inside* our brain. Somewhere within our brain we are creating a 'visual stage' built from signals from our eyes, memories, expectations, etc.

Now when we listen to a stereo hi-fi system we sit equidistant between the two speakers and an appropriate distance away. And because our left and right ears receive different signals, our auditory cortex is able to reconstruct a *sound stage* of the music that has spatial breadth and depth. But this sound stage does not appear to be inside our heads—it appears to exist in the space occupied by the speakers. However, we know that this cannot be true. Just like our sense of vision, our sense of sound must occur within our brain. What actually happens is that, spatially, our sound stage overlays our visual stage, and sounds are accurately correlated with physical objects.

Research by Plenge (1974) showed that the pinnae were actually responsible for externalizing the sound stage. For when the influence of the pinnae was removed, the sound stage appeared to be internal, rather than external. This is easily demonstrated by the action of modern lightweight headphones that 'plug' into the middle ear. When wearing these headphones, one is aware that the stereo sound stage exists between the ears, and does not have any external existence.

It was quickly realized that if the signals driving a set of headphones could be artificially modified to simulate the spectral shaping by the head and the pinnae, it would be possible to externalize the sound stage. Indeed this is the case, and the signal processing functions required are called *Head-Related Transfer Functions* (HRTFs). For accuracy, the HRTFs take into account the shape of the upper torso. Furthermore, as the shape of our ears, head and shoulders are all different; we each possess a personal set of HRTFs.

Now the reason for explaining this process is that VR systems are often equipped with stereo headphones that can be used to communicate sound signals from virtual objects. If these signals are not pre-processed by HRTFs the sound stage will appear within the user's head rather than superimposed upon the external visual stage. However, the HRTFs will probably be based upon some generic set of pinnae, head and torso measurements, and the effect is only approximate.

Tactile

The tactile senses are important in VR as it would be useful to touch virtual objects, feel them vibrate, and react to their weight. Obviously, such sensations have to be simulated, and it will be useful to understand some of the sensory mechanisms involved.

Touch receptors

Touch, pressure, and vibration are *somatic senses* that are nervous mechanisms for collecting sensory data from our body. All three sensations are detected by similar types of receptors: touch receptors are found in the skin or in local tissue; pressure receptors lie within deeper tissues and respond to tissue deformation; and the sensation of vibration is detected by both touch and pressure receptors.

Guyton (1991) classifies the somatic sensations as follows:

> "*Exteroreceptive sensations* are those from the surface of the body. *Proprioceptive sensations* are those having to do with the physical state of the body, including position sensations, tendon and muscle sensations, pressure sensations from the bottom of the feet, and even the sensation of

equilibrium, which is generally considered to be a 'special' sensation rather than a somatic sensation.

Visceral sensations are those from the viscera of the body; in using this term one usually refers specifically to sensations from the internal organs.

The *deep sen*sations are those that come from the deep tissues, such as from fasciae, muscles, bone, and so forth. These include mainly 'deep' pressure, pain and vibration."

The tactile senses present much more of a challenge to VR technology than any of the other senses. For if we are to stimulate the tactile senses we have to find ways of stimulating the skin and deep muscle tissue. The tactile receptors comprise free nerve endings that are found all over the surface of the skin and within certain tissues. The slightest breeze or a fly landing for a fraction of a second can activate these.

Where spatial discrimination is required and touch sensation is vital, a receptor called *Meissner's corpuscles* is used. These are found especially on the lips and fingertips. Hairy areas of the skin contain *expanded tip tactile receptors* which adapt slowly to their stimuli—this allows them to monitor touch conditions that remain over a period of time.

Each hair on our skin has a nerve fiber attached to its base called the *hair end-organ*. These are stimulated just before our skin makes contact with a foreign object. Deeper inside the skin and tissue are located *Ruffini's end-organs* that respond to continuous states of deformation, continuous touch conditions, and pressure signals. And finally, *pacinian corpuscles* are located just beneath the skin and deep within the fascial tissues; these are sensitive to tissue vibrations.

With such an array of receptors, it is going to be difficult to stimulate them using electronic and mechanical technologies. Even the act of wearing a glove containing active pressure pads will stimulate the skin receptors. We may be able to sense the vibrations emanating from the glove, but it cannot be compared to holding or touching a real object.

If we are to feel the weight of a virtual object, somehow forces must be transmitted to our arms. But it is not just our arms that react to the weight of something, it is our whole body. Even our legs and the soles of our feet respond to the weight.

Equilibrium

In the previous section on hearing we saw that the inner ear houses the cochlea, which converts sound pressure waves into nerve signals. The inner ear is also the home for the *vestibular system*, which is the sense for equilibrium. The vestibular system informs the brain whether we are standing upright or leaning to one side; whether we are stationary or accelerating; and in general, helps the brain understand our relationship with the ground. However, our ability to stand upright and maintain balance is also supported by complementary systems of muscles that respond to the pull of gravity.

The spinal cord connects to the brain at the brain stem, which is responsible for controlling various motor and sensory functions such as equilibrium, eye movement, gastrointestinal function, automatic body movements, respiration and control of the cardiovascular system. In general, these primitive functions can operate without any intervention from the higher levels of the brain. It is also interesting to note that when we loose equilibrium—for whatever reason—these motor functions become excited; heart and respiration rate changes, vision becomes unstable, and our stomachs respond with dramatic effect! But more of this later.

The vestibular apparatus

The *vestibular apparatus* functions by detecting the motion of fluid stored in various chambers and ducts as shown in Fig. 4.4. The *utricle* and *saccule* chambers are responsible for measuring the head's orientation relative to the Earth's gravitational field. They achieve this by monitoring the excitation of small hairs by a sticky liquid that moves whenever we bend our head forwards, backwards or sideways.

The three *semicircular ducts* are hollow semicircular bones organized at 90° to one another, that enables them to sense motion in three dimensions. When we rotate our head, liquid inside the ducts is displaced and small hairs are excited, but within a second or so, the liquid catches up with the motion of the duct. Similarly, when we stop our head rotating, the same hairs are excited. Thus the semicircular ducts act as accelerometers and are sensitive to about 1° per sec. per sec.; but they do *not* detect if equilibrium has been lost. Because of their sensitivity, their true role is to 'advise' the brain that equilibrium *will* be lost if action is not taken. This gives the brain time to respond with appropriate muscular adjustments throughout the body, reflexive arm gestures, and rotation of the eyes to retain a stable image. It is a beautiful arrangement, but for some, it is easily disturbed.

Motion sickness

Many people are sensitive to certain types of motion and suffer from the effects of motion sickness. This begins with a strange sense of 'something's wrong'; moves through stages of sweating, nausea, loss of balance and can eventually end with vomiting, followed by a long period of 'being out of action'. All of this is attributed to a loss of equilibrium.

Seasickness is a common complaint when sailing on rough seas. For some people though, the sea does not have to be particularly rough—just loosing sight of the horizon for a few seconds is sufficient to induce nausea. Other people are ill when flying, being driven in a car, or sitting the wrong way in a moving train. But it is also known that people who spend too long in flight simulators, especially those systems with panoramic displays and no motion platform, suffer similar problems. Some pilots who undergo long training sessions in dome simulators report 'out-of-body' experiences, loss of balance, and general disorientation, and require a good 24-hour period of readjustment.

Implications for VR

Users of VR systems must also be aware of the problems introduced by the technology of HMDs, immersive displays, motion platforms, and real-time computer graphics, as they can all unwittingly induce motion sickness. Take, for example, HMDs. These cut the user from the real visual world, and thus isolate them from landmarks such as the ground plane, and the horizon. A HMD's optical system must be aligned correctly. If, for example, the right hand image is slightly rotated relative to the left-hand image, one eye will attempt to resolve the situation by rotating about its gaze axis. This not only causes eyestrain, but also can induce serious nausea.

Large immersive panoramic displays can envelop our horizontal field of view, and can induce motion sickness when viewing certain types of graphics. This is because these displays stimulate our peripheral field of view where motion cues are detected. If the real-time images involve rapid rotations and sudden stops and starts, motion sickness can be induced within seconds.

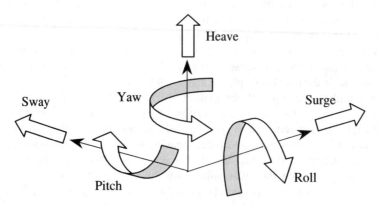

Fig. 4.6 *A 6 DOF axial system.*

The motion platforms used in flight and entertainment simulators are able to slide along and rotate about three axes; such movements are called *Degrees Of Freedom* (DOF). Some motion platforms are constrained to 3 DOF, whereas others are unconstrained and possess 6 DOF. Fig. 4.6 shows the three axes oriented such that one-axis points forward, another points upwards, and the third points sideways. The rotational movements are called *roll, yaw* and *pitch* respectively. Linear movements along these axes are called *surge, heave* and *sway* respectively. Now, normal unconstrained motion involves 6 DOF, but if a motion platform only possesses 3 DOF, people sensitive to motion sickness are the first to notice. For example, a low-cost motion platform may be constrained to roll, pitch and heave, but are used with simulator ride experiences containing all 6 degrees of freedom. Thus during the ride our vestibular system detects roll, pitch and heave, our eyes detect roll, pitch, yaw, surge, heave and sway, and the stomach reacts accordingly! The conflict between equilibrium signals provided by the vestibular system and the motion cues from the visual system are thought to be the cause of such motion sickness.

Fortunately, not everyone suffers from motion sickness, but one cannot ignore the effect it has, and it is possible to minimize its effects with a little thought.

Summary

Even from this brief overview of human factors it is obvious that it is going to be extremely difficult to find a range of technologies that will mimic the senses of sight, sound, touch and balance. But if we remember that the objective of VR is not to replicate our experience of the real world, but to make things as realistic and useful as possible, then solutions are within our grasp.

Engineers will not want to tap a virtual component with a virtual hammer to hear what sound it makes, neither will they want to lift up a virtual car engine to estimate its weight. Similarly it will not be necessary to feel the temperature of a virtual tractor when its engine is running, nor will it be necessary to simulate heat haze, exhaust fumes and the vibrations and rattles made by virtual components.

If VR is to be used by a wide community of people it must:

- Be easy to use.
- Accommodate a wide variety of human sizes.
- Not cause fatigue.
- Not induce nausea.
- Not require long periods of adaptation.

It is very easy to upset our sensory systems. Even wearing reading glasses that are optically too strong can cause fatigue and disturb our sense of balance; therefore great care is needed in the design of HMDs.

Although sound is a useful complementary cue, it does not have to be as accurate as the visual channel. Simple, relevant sounds relayed over headphones are often more than adequate to introduce an added sense of realism for most projects. The same is probably true for touch and haptic forces. Yes, it would be nice to feel a virtual object when our finger tips first make contact, but there is no need for such sophistication if there is no real added value.

Perhaps the one sense that requires careful attention above all is equilibrium. It is quickly disturbed, especially by conflicting cues from the visual channel and vestibular system. And it is rather unfortunate that somewhere along the line, the stomach became hardwired within the sensory communication network!

The simulation industry has for many years been able to work within the human body's sensory envelope when designing training simulators; therefore it should not be too difficult for the VR community to devise equally compatible systems.

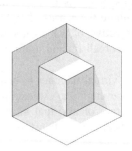

5

VR Hardware

Introduction

In this chapter I want to describe the hardware used in various VR systems. Such hardware is evolving very fast, and rather than concentrate upon specific manufacturer's models, I will describe generic devices and their operational characteristics and refer to specific systems where appropriate. Those readers who wish to discover the technical details of commercially available systems can look at manufacturer's Web sites listed in Appendix E.

Under this heading of hardware we will look at the computers used for VR, tracking technology, input devices, glasses, displays, and audio. It will not be an exhaustive list, but sufficient for the reader to appreciate the range of technologies available.

Before we start though, it is time to consolidate our ideas about three terms that have been introduced in previous chapters: refresh rate, update rate and lag or latency. These terms are used in association with tracking systems, image generators, and entire VR systems.

Refresh rate

Refresh rate is associated with some form of display device such as a television, computer monitor, or HMD. It defines how often the screen is refreshed with an image—which may be the same image, or a new image. In television technology an image is composed of two parts called fields: one field consists of the odd rasters, and another field consists of the even rasters. This is called *interlacing*. Fig. 5.1 shows the two fields formed by a television Cathode Ray Tube (CRT). The solid horizontal line is the raster where the image is being refreshed, and the diagonal dashed line represents the fly-back part where the beam is blanked and repositioned for the next raster. Interlacing the odd field followed by the even field keeps the image refreshed. For video technology there is a field and frame refresh rate, and Table 5.1 shows these speeds for the UK's PAL coding system and the USA's NTSC coding system.

The reason for dividing an image into two parts is to minimize the frequency bandwidth of the broadcast signal, and to reduce flicker by maximizing the refresh rate.

Table 5.1 Field and frame rates for the USA and UK.

	USA (NTSC)	UK (PAL)
Field rate	60 Hz	50 Hz
Frame rate	30 Hz	25 Hz

A television receives its new images from the signals detected by its aerial, and as there are a specified number of fields transmitted, all the television circuitry has to do is keep everything synchronized. However, a computer monitor has its image maintained inside a portion of memory that is updated whenever the computer is instructed.

Today, most computer monitors are non-interlaced, and the entire frame is refreshed at a speed that causes minimum flicker, and is in the order of 72 Hz.

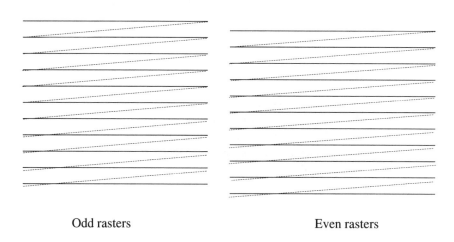

Odd rasters   Even rasters

Fig. 5.1 The two fields that make a video frame.

Update rate

The update rate is the rate at which the *content* of the image is updated. For example, in television, a video camera samples a scene at the video rates shown in Table 5.1, which means that the update rate equals the refresh rate. But in a computer, the update rate is determined by the speed at which software is executed. For example, if a computer can only execute the renderer program at 10 Hz, there will only be 10 different images seen every second, but the monitor will still attempt to refresh the screen at its refresh rate. And say it takes exactly 0.5 seconds to render an image, and the refresh rate is 72 Hz: the monitor will display the first image 36 times and the second image 36 times.

Latency

Latency or lag is the time delay between an event occurring and its observation. In the context of television, the time between an event recorded by a camera and seen on a television screen is a very small fraction of a second. This is because the signals coming from a video camera pass through cables and electronic circuits at a speed approaching the speed of light (300,000 Km/s). And when a television transmitter radiates these signals, they pass through space at the speed of light until intercepted by an aerial. Thus even if the signal has to travel 100 Km, there is only a delay of 0.0003 seconds!

In computers anything can happen: I can touch a key, and a letter appears on the screen virtually instantaneously; but if the operating system suddenly decides to auto-save my file to hard disk, I might wait four or five seconds before the screen responds to keyboard activities. In such an environment the latency varies according to how busy the processor is.

In a VR system, latency can be the time that elapses between a tracking system detecting a new head position and the user seeing a corresponding image on the display. Fig. 5.2 shows how the process of recording the position of the user's head to the display of a corresponding image can be visualized as a sequential pipeline of activities.

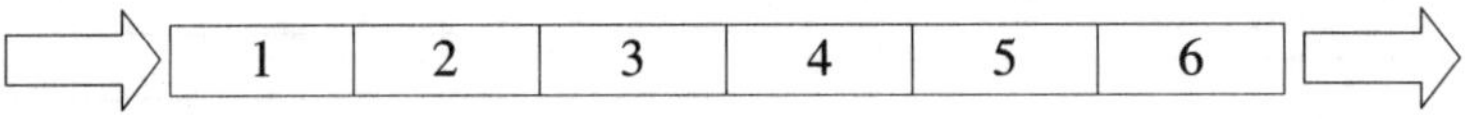

1	Detect new head position
2	Convert position to Cartesian coordinates
3	Relay to host VR computer
4	Update renderer with new position
5	Calculate new perspective view
6	Render new image

Fig. 5.2 Pipeline of activities between head tracking and display of image.

For simplicity, let us assume that all six activities are running at 50 Hz. This means that each activity in the pipeline is taking 0.02 seconds (1/50) to process a new piece of data. Therefore, the total latency is 6 x 0.02 which equals 0.12 seconds. Thus, it is the number of sequential stages that introduces latency.

These terms: refresh rate, update rate and latency will surface again in the following hardware descriptions.

Computers

Computers come in all shapes and sizes: from the humble PC to the massively parallel supercomputer used for simulating global weather patterns, or cosmological 'big bangs'. Today, however, virtually all computers are able to create pictures of some sort, and are therefore potential candidates as a VR platform. But, every computer has processing limitations, which ultimately dictates the complexity of 3D images they can manipulate. We will now take a brief look at PCs, graphics workstations, supercomputers and image generators.

PC

We saw in Chapter 3 that a VR application really stretches a computer to the very limit. In some instances it has to hold the 3D database, produce real-time, shaded, stereoscopic views of the VE, support audio, simulate animated sequences, support user interaction, and perhaps work collaboratively with other users. Such a range of tasks can easily exceed the operational envelope of many PCs, but if we are prepared to lower our expectations slightly, a PC is able to cope with many simple VEs.

Most PCs are fitted with some sort of graphics facility to support multimedia applications and the display of 2D and 3D graphics. Although such PCs can display simple VEs, high-performance graphics boards are required to provide the real-time display of large databases. The specification of such boards includes parameters such as:

- range of resolutions
- large on-board texture memory
- perspective correct texture mapping
- sub-pixel and sub-texel positioning
- texture morphing
- Gouraud modulated textures
- video texture mapping
- anti-aliasing
- number of textured triangles rendered per second
- sustained pixel fill rate
- NTSC/PAL standards
- per-pixel fog, smoke and haze effects.

The resolution for most HMDs is in the order of 640h × 480v, whereas for monitors it is typically 1280h × 1024v. Most graphics boards can cope with this range of resolution, but because the on-board texture memory is currently around 4MB the range of displayed colors is dependent upon resolution. For example, the Obsidian range of boards display 256, 65K and 16.7 million colors at a resolution of 640 × 480; but only 256 colors at 128 × 1024.

Rendering speeds are measured in terms of how many pixels can be written per second and/or millions of textured triangles per second, with most boards currently approaching a fill rate of 100 mega-pixels/second and exceeding 1 million triangles per second. However, one must be careful when comparing board specifications, as triangles are measured in different ways. To estimate the maximum rate at which the computer can update the viewing of the VE (the *update rate*) we divide the rendering speed by the number of displayed triangles. For example, if the rendering speed is 1 million triangles per second, and the VE contains 20,000 visible triangles, the maximum update rate is approximately 50Hz, which is more than adequate for any VR application. But this is for a single view of the VE. If left and right views are required the performance will reduce to 25Hz, which is still adequate.

Another important feature of graphics boards concerns the software they support. Again, a product like Obsidian offers supports:

- Gemini Technology OpenGVS™
- Datapath RealiMation™
- Silicon Graphics® Cosmo™
- Criterion® RenderWare™
- Argonaut BRender™
- Numerical Design NETIMMERSE™
- NDimension SimStudio™
- Newfire Torch™
- Hybrid SurRender™
- Sense8® WorldToolkit™
- SciTech MGL™
- Soft Reality SoftVR™

In the field of computer games—which must be accepted as a form of VR—general purpose PCs are becoming an important commercial platform. And publishers of computer games have already realized that they must supply games that run on PCs as well as the various game stations. Currently, there is a strong movement towards Windows NT PCs, and as the clock speed of such machines exceed 500 MHz, it is inevitable they will become a major force in future VR systems. They are already starting to appear and enable users to configure a powerful VR system simply by plugging various boards to support VR peripherals such as HMDs, mice and trackers. The advantage of this approach is that the PC still remains a PC, and can be used for all of the normal functions of word processing, spreadsheets, slide presentations, etc., as well as supporting VR when needed.

One problem that everyone faces when purchasing a computer, especially a graphics computer, is its speed relative to other machines. One cannot go by the main processor's clock speed as this says nothing about the internal architecture, data bandwidths, buffers, etc. To help with this problem Superscape has created a Web site called www.3Dbenchmark.com that provides a benchmark for testing the graphics performance of VR systems. One simply logs onto the site and starts the benchmark process. Your computer is then given a range of tasks to evaluate its speed at texture mapping, transparency, lighting, Gouraud and Phong shading, fog, etc. For each task the computer's update rate is measured, from which a single update rate is calculated. By subjecting other computers to the same test it is possible to compare their graphics performance.

Graphics workstation

Computer graphics workstations have always played an important role in supporting VR applications. Their cost varies considerably and they have always outperformed PCs, but today's Windows NT PCs offer comparable performance at a reduced cost, and are vigorously challenging this position.

Computer graphics workstations operate within a UNIX operating system, and although they may work with processor clock speeds that are comparable with PCs, it is their internal data channels and architecture that provides the added performance. The UNIX operating system provides an ideal environment for developing software, and given the choice, programmers will always opt for a workstation rather than a PC to develop code.

Graphics workstations are also specified in terms of the rendering speed, and although, they provide extra performance, it is not inevitable that this will always be the case. Considerable effort is currently going into the design of more powerful 3D graphics boards, and as their market share increases, the distinction between PCs and workstations is becoming increasingly blurred.

Supercomputer

Certain types of supercomputers generally manufactured by Silicon Graphics, Inc. are often used for high-end VR applications. Such machines are used because of the superior rendering speeds, often measured in tens of millions of triangles per second. The rendering process introduces environment and texture mapping and can even include shadows. They are used for the real-time display of very large VEs and in displays where three projectors create a panoramic image, or in a CAVE.

Apart from their rendering performance, their computational power can also be harnessed to support event simulation within the VE. But as one might expect, such performance has an associated higher price tag.

Image generator

Finally, Image Generators (IGs) are specifically designed to produce real-time images, and are widely used throughout the simulation industry. One very important application is in civilian and military flight simulators.

Evans & Sutherland are world famous for their IGs and produced their first real-time Line Drawing System in 1968. Today, they produce a range of systems including their Harmony NT based product, the compact Liberty IG (Fig. 5.3) and the ESIG range of IGs.

The ESIG-4500 family of IGs can be configured in many ways: an ESIG-4530 can have up to 16 independent eye-points, and each independent eye-point can have up to 8 channels. A 3-channel system, for example, would support a 150° panoramic screen display, with each channel responsible for a 50° sector of the screen. Standard and optional features of an ESIG-4500 include:

- Up to 8300 polygons per channel processor at 60 Hz.
- Thousands of moving models.
- Depth buffering.
- MIP texture.
- Texture animation for dynamic special effects such as smoke and dust.
- Light lobes that depict own-vehicle lighting.
- Mission functions such as height above terrain, collision detection, laser range-finding, and line-of-sight ranging.
- Calligraphic lights.

- Layered fog effects.
- Steerable searchlights.
- Independent illumination sources such as flares.
- Dynamic sea states which provide a 3D ocean surface that can be controlled in real time to produce different wave heights, spacing and direction of movement and that interacts realistically with objects such as ships and life rafts.
- Weapons effects.
- Horizon depression to accurately depict the Earth's curvature at higher altitudes.

It is obvious from such a state-of-the-art specification that the simulation industry is well served, and demonstrates what can be achieved with today's technology.

Fig. 5.3 The E&S Liberty IG. (Courtesy Evans & Sutherland)

Tracking

In recent years many technologies have emerged to capture the motion of humans. Some of this technology is used in computer animation and some for VR systems. In computer animation character animation is particularly difficult, especially when a high level of realism is required, and although scripting and key-frame animation can obtain good results, motion capture is even better.

In VR, tracking technology is required to monitor the real-time position and orientation of the user's head and hand. In some applications the user's arm is required and in some instances the entire body. The technologies currently used in VR include mechanical, optical, ultrasonic and magnetic, and Appendix C lists some popular systems.

Latency and the update rate are two important parameters associated with trackers, and out of the two it is the latter that is most important. The update rate determines the time taken between measuring a position and its availability to the VR software. If this becomes too high, say 100 ms; it makes interaction and navigation very tiresome.

Mechanical

A simple mechanical tracker can take the form of mechanical arm jointed at the shoulder, elbow and wrist. When one end is fixed, the 3D position of the other end is readily calculated by measuring the joint angles using suitable transducers. The electro-mechanical nature of the device gives it high accuracy and low latency, but its active volume is restricted.

Mechanical trackers are very useful when integrated with a hand-held display. Fakespace, Inc., in particular, has pioneered this form of technology with products such as their BOOM3C, FS^2, MEDVIEW and PUSH. See Fig. 5.4.

Optical

One popular form of motion capture employs infrared video cameras that record the movement of a person. Attached to the person is a collection of markers in the form of small balls fixed to critical joints. When the moving person is illuminated with infrared light the marker balls are readily detected within the video images. As the system depends upon line of sight, the orientation of the cameras must be such to ensure that the markers are always visible. The positions of the markers within the video images are identified by host software, and triangulated to compute their 3D position in space. If the 3D points are stored as a file they can be used at some later date to animate the joints of a computer-animated character to great effect. If, however, the 3D points are input to a real-time computer system they can be used to control some virtual character.

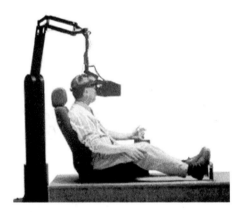

Fig. 5.4 *A Fakespace BOOM display. (Courtesy Fakespace)*

One popular motion capture system is the ExpertVision HiRES system by Motion Analysis Corporation. It supports up to 125 markers and up to 10 cameras, with frame rates from 60 to 240 fps. The system can cope with spins and flips, and compensates for blocked markers by using spline curves and redundant markers.

In Japan, the ExpertVision system has been used to animate the virtual singer *Kyoko*. Kyoko is the brainchild of HoriPro, a Japanese talent agency, and has been modeled from 40,000 polygons with incredible detail. The virtual singer is expected to have a long and commercial career if she can be exported around the world.

The other system from Motion Analysis is their FaceTracker. This captures facial expressions by monitoring the motion of small markers attached to the user's face. As the user's head is also tracked, the data can be used to control the dynamics of an online virtual head. Anticipated markets for this technology are in computer animation, film special effects, 3D Web sites, real-time cartoons, etc.

Ultrasonic

As the name suggests, ultrasonic trackers employ ultrasonic sound to locate the position of the user's head. They are generally used for *fish-tank VR* where a user is seated in front of a monitor screen, but gets the impression of seeing a volume of space in the form of a fish tank inside the monitor. The ultrasonic tracker is placed on top of the monitor and records the user's head movements. The signal is sent to the display software, which in turn updates the image with an appropriate perspective view.

The advantages are that it is simple, effective, accurate and low cost, but it is restricted to working within a small volume, it is sensitive to temperature, and depends upon line of sight.

Electromagnetic

Electromagnetic tracking technology is very popular and is used to monitor the position and orientation of the user's head and hand. The system employs a device called a *source* that emits an electromagnetic field, and a *sensor* that detects the radiated field. The source, which can be no bigger than a 2 inch cube can be placed on a table or fixed to a ceiling. The sensor is even smaller and is readily attached to a HMD or fitted within a 3D mouse.

Fig. 5.5 The Polhemus Fastrak tracker (Courtesy Polhemus)

When the sensor is moved about in space it detects different magnetic fields that encode its position and orientation. When the decoded signals are relayed back to the host VR computer they modify the displayed view or the position of a virtual 3D cursor. The latency of these systems is very low—often less than 10 ms—but another parameter to watch is the update rate, as this determines the number of samples returned to the host computer.

Because electromagnetic fields are used, there are no line of sight restrictions, however the active volume is restricted to a few cubic meters, and large metallic objects readily disturb the fields.

Polhemus market a variety of products such as STAR*TRAK, ULTRATRAK, FASTRACK (Fig. 5.5), ISOTRAK and INSIDETRAK. The 3SPACE FASTRAK accepts four receivers for each transmitter, with a total of 8 transmitters (32 receivers) and is widely used for VR applications. Its accuracy is 0.03 inches RMS, a resolution of 0.0002 in./in. and a latency of 4 ms. Its standard working range is just over 3 m but can be extended to 10 m with an optional LONG RANDER transmitter. The update rate is quoted as 120 updates/sec. divided by the number of receivers. In the case of a head and hand tracked system (two receivers) the update is a respectable 60 Hz.

Fig. 5.6 *The Polhemus Ultratrak Pro.*
(Courtesy Polhemus)

Polhemus have also harnessed electromagnetic technology for full motion capture over very large areas. Their Ultratrak Pro system illustrated in Fig. 5.6, is capable of tracking up to 32 individual receivers, over a radius of 15 ft., at an update rate of 60 Hz. If a higher update rate is required, 16 receivers can be monitored at 120 Hz. The position and orientation of each sensor is measured using low-frequency electromagnetic waves that do not require line-of-sight operation.

Where complete freedom is required, a Polhemus Star*Belt can be used to capture up to 20 minutes of motion data, that can be used for real-time playback after the session. Plate 2 shows a motion capture session using a Polhemus motion capture system.

Inertial

Inertial trackers use the Earth's gravitational or magnetic field to measure orientation, and because they cannot currently determine position their application is limited in VR. See Hollands (1995) for a detailed survey.

Input devices

The input devices normally associated with a VR system are the 3D mouse and glove. Other esoteric devices are being developed but only exist as research tools, and are therefore omitted from this *essential* overview.

3D Mouse

A 3D mouse is a hand-held device containing a tracker sensor and some buttons, and is used for navigating or picking objects within a VE. In navigation the orientation of the mouse can be used to control the forward speed, whilst the user's gaze direction dictates the direction of travel. For example, tilting the mouse forward could initiate a forward movement, and holding it vertical stops the motion. It would be foolish to arrange that leaning the mouse backwards cause the user to fly backwards; it would not only be very confusing but could easily induce motion sickness.

Fig. 2.6 shows Logitech's Spacemouse, Spacetec's Spaceball, and Virtual Presence's Spacestick.

Polhemus provide another type of input device called a 3BALL that works with one of Polhemus' sources. It is a hand-held 2.4 in. diameter ball weighing 5 ounces, connected to the host computer via a cable. Inside the ball is a small sensor that measures position and orientation, and a small surface switch provides both tactile and audio feedback.

Gloves

Because hand gestures were an intuitive way of directing actions within early VR systems, gloves became very popular. Unfortunately, they were expensive and earned a reputation for unreliability.

A simple interactive glove is made from a lightweight material into which transducers are sewn to measure finger joint angles. The transducers can be strain gauges or fiber optics that change their physical characteristics when they are stretched. Most modern gloves are very accurate and are used to communicate hand gestures such as pointing and grasping to the host software, and in some cases return tactile signals to the user's hand.

Whilst the glove monitors the orientation of the fingers, an extra tracker on the wrist monitors the position and orientation of the hand. Together, they enable a complete virtual hand to be animated within a VE.

Fig. 2.9 shows the CyberGlove from Virtual Technologies. This has a tactile feedback option in the form of small vibrotactile stimulators on each finger and the palm of the glove. These stimulators can create patterns of pulses and vibrations (125Hz max.) to confirm collisions with virtual objects.

Output devices

Force feedback sensors

Many modern cars tend to isolate the driver from forces that could be transmitted through the steering wheel. Such cars deprive the driver of valuable information relating to the car's stability and the way it 'sits' on the road. Fortunately, it is still possible to buy cars that let the driver know exactly what the suspension is doing, and what is happening where the tires meet the road surface.

In civilian planes external forces are often fed back to the pilot through the flight controls, and are so important that they are replicated within a flight simulator. Thus when a pilot undertakes a banking maneuver or lands on a virtual runway, the host computer outputs appropriate signals that are turned into forces with the aid of electric motors. The overall effect is highly realistic.

The devices that return force information to a VR user are known as *haptic* devices as they provide some form of sensory feedback through the tactile senses. Thus it is possible to touch, weigh and grasp virtual objects. However, we cannot feel, weigh and grasp a virtual apple in the way we can a real apple—for the sensations from the virtual apple have to be communicated through some mechanical device. One way of appreciating the difference is to imagine an apple hidden inside a closed box. If we had a stick that could be inserted through a small aperture, we could feel the apple using the stick. We could sense its hard surface, its mass, and even its inertia when it rolled on the stick. It is these forces that can be fed back to a VR user through an appropriate 'force stick'.

If we had robotic technology in the form of a mechanical glove, it could be arranged that every finger joint could be activated by a small electric motor. Thus when we attempted to close our fingers together, appropriate signals could be sent to the motors to restrict our finger movement. When connected to a VE, it would be possible to grasp virtual objects and feel our fingers restrained from squashing the object.

If we wish to feel the weight of a virtual object our robot arm will have to apply forces that simulate the action of gravity. Thus we will have to exert a force upward to overcome the effective weight of virtual object.

Table 5.2 *Technical characteristics of the Super Expanded Workspace PHANToM.*

Super Expanded Workspace PHANToM		
Minimal position resolution	>1000 dpi	0.02 mm
Workspace	16x23x33 in	42x59x82 cm.
Backdrive friction	0.75 oz	0.02 N
Maximum exertable force	4.9 lbf	22N
Closed loop stiffness	5.7 lbs/in	1 N/mm
Inertia (apparent mass at tip)	<0.34 lbm	<150g
Footprint	8x8 in	20x20 cm

One very effective haptic device is the PHANToM Haptic Interface System from Sensable, Inc. A series of products that include the Standard Workspace, Expanded Workspace and the Super Expanded Workspace provide a range of solutions to implement a haptic interface. The top-of-the-range product provides a working volume of 16×22×33 inches in which a haptic response is available to the user via a thimble or stylus. The user places a finger inside the thimble or holds a stylus to feel the feedback force. The characteristics of the device are shown in Table 5.2.

Force feedback is required in VR systems for molecular modeling systems, surgical training and training simulators for heavy machinery. And because each application has unique requirements, bespoke hardware is often required. However, a variety of joysticks are available that can provide forces to oppose a user's commands. Other more esoteric structures are still in research labs around the world, and we will have to wait some time before they surface as commercial products.

Glasses

Glasses with red and green filters are an excellent way of creating a 3D effect from a single overprinted red and green image (*anaglyph*). Similarly, glasses fitted with polarized filters can create stunning effects when looking at films projected through polarized light. Building upon the success of these simple techniques glasses have been developed to create 3D images when looking at a single monitor screen. An ideal solution however, should not involve glasses, but such technology is still being developed.

Shutter glasses

If we display alternately the left and right-eye images of a VE on a monitor, the end result would be a blurred overlay. But if we could keep our left eye open when the left image was displayed, and similarly for the right eye with its image, we would obtain a 3D effect. This is impossible unaided because the images are switching to fast. However, we could get a pair of glasses to do the switching for us, and such glasses are called *shutter glasses*. The glasses operate by making the left or right-hand lens opaque or transparent using liquid crystal technology, and they receive a synchronizing signal from an infrared unit placed on top of the monitor. When the left image is displayed on the monitor a signal is sent to the glasses to shut the right-hand lens, and *vice versa* for the right image. The end result is a very realistic 3D effect that can be enhanced even further by including head tracking. There are however, two slight disadvantages: attenuation in brightness and ghosting. LCD filters are not perfect transmitters of light, and because they are unable to switch off completely, it is possible of one eye to see the other eye's image and cause ghosting.

CrystalEyes are the best-known shutter glasses for use in VR systems. They work with PCs, Macs and workstations, and many computers come equipped with a jack point. Fig. 5.7 shows the glasses, and a technical specification is shown in Table 5.3.

Plate 1 *Simulator ride "Mission on Mars". (Image courtesy of The Cupboard)*

Plate 2 *Polhemus tracking technology. (Image courtesy of Polhemus)*

Plate 3 *External view of a Viper. (Image courtesy of James Hans)*

Plate 4 *Internal view of a Viper. (Image courtesy of James Hans)*

Plate 5 *Radiosity view of a day-lit museum using the LightWorks rendering system. (Image courtesy of LightWork Design)*

Plate 6 *Radiosity view of a lit aircraft interior using the LightWorks rendering system. (Image courtesy of LightWork Design)*

Plate 7 *A virtual airliner flies over San Francisco bay on a clear summer day. The city is modeled with geospecific texture derived from photographs. (ESIG-4500 image courtesy of Evans & Sutherland)*

Plate 8 *Virtual EFA 2000s fly over a farming area with nearby suburbs. Visibility is good, but the haze band in the distance shows that it isn't a perfectly clear day. (ESIG 4500 image courtesy of Evans & Sutherland)*

Plate 9 *Virtual fog combined with photoderived texture creates highly realistic scenes with real-world visibility parameters. (ESIG 4500 image courtesy of Evans & Sutherland)*

Plate 10 *Four views of a virtual tractor. (Images courtesy of Division)*

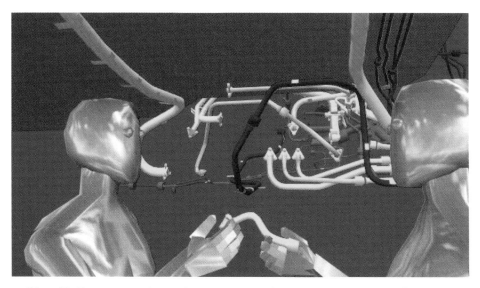

Plate 11 *Two mannequins exchanging a virtual pipe. (Image courtesy of Division)*

Plate 12 Internal view of an F1 car. (Image courtesy of Division)

Plate 13 CAD component in a VE. (Image courtesy of Division)

Plate 14 *A view of virtual Venice. (Image courtesy of Superscape)*

Plate 15 *A view of virtual Venice. (Image courtesy of Superscape)*

Plate 16 The S2I interactive simulator. (Image courtesy of Thomson Entertainment)

Plate 17 Caister Murdoch gas compression platform using Cadcentre's Review
Reality System. (Image courtesy of Conoco / Brown & Root)

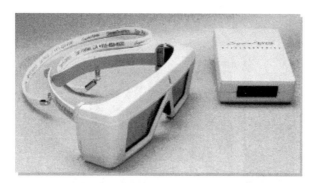

Fig. 5.7 *CrystalEyes. (Courtesy Stereographics)*

Table 5.3 *Technical specification for the CrystalEyes shutter glasses.*

CrystalEyes	
Transmittance	32% (typical)
Dynamic range	1000:1 min
Close time	0.2 ms (typical)
Open time	2.8 ms (typical)
Field rate	90 to 160 fields/sec
Weight	3.3 oz (93 g)
Batteries	Two 3V lithium

Displays

Display technology is central to any VR system, and to a certain extent is helping to classify the emerging configurations. And although real-time systems started with monitor based computer graphics systems, it was the HMD that paved the way to what we now know as immersive VR. But since the emergence of HMDs other devices have appeared such as BOOM displays, CAVEs, virtual tables and panoramic screens.

3D screen

Stereographics manufacture a polarizing panel that transforms a projection system or computer monitor into a 3D display. Fig. 5.8 shows the screen attached to a monitor. The ZScreen operates somewhat like shutter glasses: when a left image is displayed on the monitor the image is polarized, say horizontally, and when the right image is displayed the polarization is vertical. Now if the viewer is wearing a pair of polarized glasses, their left and right eyes will see a sequence of corresponding left and right views of a scene.

The ZScreen has proved very useful for visualizing a wide variety of data sets, and because it is the screen that is active, the user simply dons a pair of passive polarized glasses.

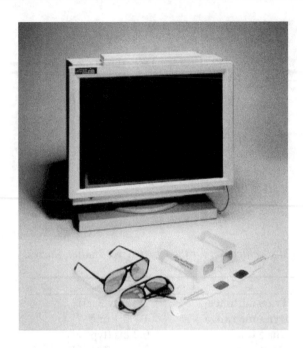

Fig. 5.8 The ZScreen. (Courtesy Stereographics)

HMD

HMDs possess a variety of characteristics such as *contrast ratio, luminance, field of view, exit pupil, eye relief* and *overlap*. The contrast ratio is the ratio of the peak luminance to the background luminance, and a value of 100:1 is typical. Luminance is a measure of a screen's brightness, and ideally should exceed 1000 cd/m². Field Of View (FOV) is a measure of the horizontal and vertical visual range of the optical system, and ideally should approach that of the human visual system. In general though, most HMDs may only provide about 60° FOV for each eye. The exit pupil is the distance the eye can deviate from the optical center of the display before the image disappears. This is in the order of 1.2 cm. Eye relief is a measure of the distance between the HMD's optical system and the user's face, and is in the order of 2 cm. And finally, overlap is a measure of the image overlap to create a stereoscopic image.

A typical HMD will contain two LCD elements viewed through infinity optics—that is to say they are collimated to infinity. The resolution is typically 640h × 480v pixels, and because one is so close to the elements, it is quite normal to discern the structure of the pixels. No doubt, as display technology improves, we will have access to higher resolutions without higher costs. It should be noted that CRT based HMDs to not suffer from this problem.

The horizontal field of view for each eye is in the order of 60°, whilst the vertical field of view is 45°, and for the user to perceive a stereoscopic effect there must be some overlap between the left and right-hand images. It must also be possible to control the focus of each eye and adjust the distance between the pupils (the inter-pupilary distance).

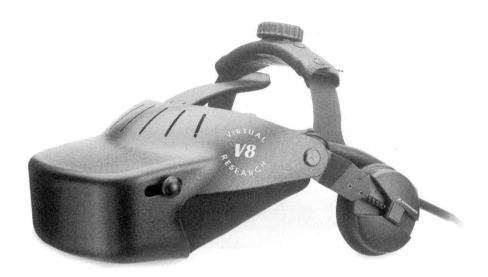

Fig. 5.9 *The Virtual Research V8 HMD. (Courtesy Virtual Research)*

Fig. 5.10 *The Virtual Research V8 Binoculars. (Courtesy Virtual Research)*

Virtual Research manufactures a range of display systems that include Cyclops, the V6 and V8 HMDs, and the V8 Binoculars. The V8 HMD is shown in Fig. 5.9, and the V8 Binoculars are shown in Fig. 5.10. The technical specification for the V8 HMD is shown in Table 5.4. Appendix B lists some commercially available HMDs.

Table 5.4 *Technical specification for the Virtual Research V8 HMD.*

Visual Research V8 HMD	
LCD size	1.3 inch diagonal Active Matrix
Resolution	640 x 480
Contrast ratio	200:1
Field-of-view	60° diagonal
Interoccular range	52 – 74 mm (adjustable)
Eye relief	10 – 30 mm (adjustable)
Stereo / mono image sources	Automatically detected
Audio	Sennheiser HD25 headphones
Weight	29 oz (821 g)
Power consumption	30 W
Cable length	13 ft (3.9 m)

BOOM

Fakespace, Inc. is particularly known for their high quality BOOM displays. These are stereo devices supported by a counterbalanced arm, and employ high resolution CRT technology. The user, who could be standing or seated maneuvers the BOOM display using side grips into some convenient view of the VE. As the BOOM is moved about, joint angles in the articulated arm are measured to enable the BOOM's 3D position to be computed. As this can be undertaken in real time, the position is supplied to the host computer to fix the viewpoint of the VE.

Retinal displays

The Human Interfaces Laboratory at the University of Washington is developing a retinal display that directs laser light direct onto the eye's retina. To date an 800 line monochrome system has been constructed and work is underway to build a full-color system that works at an even higher resolution (Tidwell *et al.*, 1995).

Panoramic screen

Military and commercial flight simulators have employed domes and panoramic displays for many years. Today, they are playing an important role in large VR centers where a group of 12 people, or so, can share the same visual experience. The screen is spherical and can be in the form of a dome, with a large horizontal and vertical field of view, or a cut down version with a restricted vertical field of view. In either format, three or more projectors are needed to cover the wide area, and for each projector an image generator channel is required to render that part of the view. Fig. 5.11 shows a system manufactured by Trimension, Ltd.

One of the problems of using multiple projectors is maintaining a consistent image quality across the screen. This calls for stable projectors where image linearity, color balance and brightness are maintained. Image linearity is needed to ensure that when an object moves from one projected image to another it occurs without distortion and without jumping rasters.

Fig. 5.11 A wide screen display system. (Courtesy Trimension)

Virtual table

Virtual tables are an excellent idea and consist of a glass or plastic screen that forms a tabletop. Inside the table a projector displays an image of a VE onto the back of the screen with alternating left and right images. With the aid of shutter glasses and head tracking one obtains an excellent 3D view of the VE. The viewpoint is determined by the viewer and is strictly a one-person system; however, it is possible for two or more people to stand close together and share a common view. It has many uses especially for military, architectural and medical applications.

Such systems were developed at the German National Computer Science and Mathematics Research Institute (GMD) and the Naval Research Laboratory and Stanford University. In 1996 Silicon Graphics, Inc. and Fakespace, Inc. announced their Immersive Workbench projected image display system at SIGGRAPH. See Fig. 5.12.

The resolution of the Workbench is 1600 × 1200 (monoscopic) and 1280 × 1024 (stereoscopic) at 120 Hz. The viewing area is 100 in. × 75 in. and can be adjusted from horizontal toward vertical. The Immersive Workbench can be applied to a wide range of applications including scale model manipulation in design projects, medical visualization, military and data visualization.

CAVE

In 1992 the University of Illinois at Chicago demonstrated their CAVE (Cave Automatic Virtual Environment) which has since developed into being a highly popular display system. A CAVE is constructed from a number of back projection screens with external projectors projecting their images. Inside the CAVE a viewer is head tracked and wears shutter glasses, so that wherever he or she looks, a stereoscopic view is seen.

The degree of immersion is very high and like the virtual table is strictly a one-person system; however, the room is normally large enough to allow other observers to share in the experience.

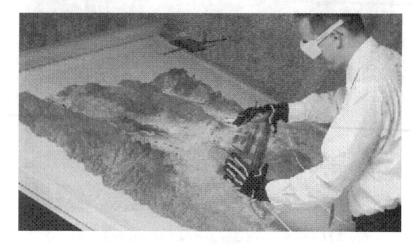

Fig. 5.12 *Fakespace's Immersive Workbench.(Courtesy Fakespace)*

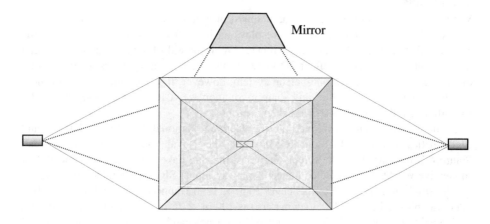

Fig. 5.13 *Projector layout of a 4-sided CAVE.*

Fig. 5.13 shows the projector layout for a 4-sided CAVE. To reduce the volume of the system, the left, right and rear projectors would have mirrors to reflect the image onto the walls, as used in the ceiling projector. The size of a CAVE is normally a 3 m cube, but can be virtually any size. A high level of immersion can be achieved with three walls, but the both the ceiling and floor can be used to totally immerse the viewer within a 3D VE.

Because magnetic tracking systems are generally used to monitor the viewer's head, the CAVEs framework must be constructed from a non-metallic material, such as wood.

Pyramid Systems, Inc. manufacture a wide variety of CAVEs, and Fig. 5.14 illustrates one of their systems being used to visualize the structure of the human brain.

Augmented reality

Augmented reality describes a VR system where computer-generated imagery is overlaid upon a normal view of the world. A head-mounted display allows the wearer to see through a visor, and with the aid of special optical elements, a transparent computer image is also seen. It requires accurate tracking technology to ensure that the two scenes are accurately aligned.

Fig. 5.14 *Visualizing 3D medical data in a CAVE.*
(Image courtesy of Pyramid Systems)

An augmented reality system could be used to train personnel to undertake a complex task. For example, to aid a worker in producing a complex wiring loom, an augmented display could be used to prompt the person with the layout for each wire. Whilst individual wires are being laid over a template, the worker sees in the display the physical path to follow.

Although such displays have been widely used by military fighter pilots, they are still being developed for commercial applications.

Audio

Although audio is important to some VR applications, not too much emphasis is given to its implementation. Sounds of engines, radios, ticking clocks, virtual telephones, mechanical machinery, and other ambient sounds are easily played back over headphones incorporated into a HMD. However, where accurate sound positioning is required various Digital Signal Processing (DSP) audio systems are available that exploit the HRTFs described in Chapter 4.

One company specializing in DSP audio systems is Lake DSP Pty. Ltd. who manufactures the Huron and CP4 systems. At the heart of both systems are DSP chips and some very clever software. For example, to simulate the acoustic properties of a virtual room, Lake's acoustic modeling software computes its *impulse response*, to capture the 3D acoustic properties of the room. This impulse response is then used to modify the frequency and phase response of any audio signal. This process is called *convolving*, and requires very high speed computing techniques, hence the use of DSPs.

Summary

At the heart of any VR system is a computer that ultimately dictates the operational envelope of the system. Its role is simple: It has to provide a real-time environment for the software coordinating the various input/output devices, as well as the standard data storage and housekeeping facilities. For some applications an ordinary PC is more than adequate to provide a cost-effective solution, but for others a workstation or supercomputer is the only option.

When connecting any peripheral to a computer one requires software to manage the interface, and it may even be necessary to incorporate an extra processing board to look after specific tasks. Some companies even provide an extra unit to integrate a HMD, tracker and 3D mouse.

As soon as one moves away from desktop VR one enters a sector where specialist knowledge is required to configure hardware and integrate the software. Real-time computer systems are complex and one should not underestimate the level of expertise required to install, support and repair them.

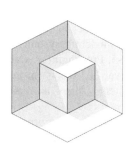

6
VR Software

Introduction

In the previous chapter we looked at the various hardware elements associated with VR systems, that included HMDs, mice, trackers, gloves, projectors, shutter glasses and host computers. Software is now required to integrate these into a coherent system that will enable a user to navigate and interact with a VE. This is no mean task, because like all computer graphics applications the software is application specific. For instance, a CAD system requires specific software tools and an appropriate interface to support the tasks required for 2D and 3D engineering design. Similarly, a 3D, computer animation system requires special tools for the modeling, animation and rendering of everything from dinosaurs to the Titanic. However, even though CAD and computer animation are both concerned with 3D objects, their requirements are totally different, and has resulted in many individual commercial software systems supporting both areas.

VR is also concerned with 3D objects, and although a CAD or computer animation system can be used to create a VE, they cannot be used to support the tasks of navigation and interaction. Special software is required to support navigation and interaction as well as collision detection, audio, level of detail, animation, simulation, etc.

By now you will have realized that VR systems can be configured in many ways and applied to dozens of different applications. At one end of the spectrum it is possible to create highly interactive 3D Web sites that can be downloaded and manipulated on a PC, and at the other end of the spectrum one can have immersive systems running on supercomputers. Although these two types of systems have different software systems, some of their requirements are common

Such software is readily available and I will try to provide a generic overview of the essential features required, and then give an overview of some commercial systems.

VR Software features

Importing models

It is pointless for any VR system to provide extensive software tools to model 3D objects or VEs—this is a complex task and many commercial modeling systems are available such as MultiGen, AutoCAD, Unigraphics II, CADDS5, Pro/Engineer, Catia, 3D Studio, Alias/Wavefront, Softimage, Lightwave, etc. However, a VR system *must* provide a mechanism for importing models from different systems—these are called *filters*.

As one might have expected, every modeling software system stores 3D information in a unique way. Furthermore, every VR system has its own internal file structure, which makes communication between different VR systems quite difficult. However, in spite of these problems, filters are available and models can be imported with minor difficulties.

The sorts of problems that arise when importing models include:

- The CAD description may not be in a polygonal format; it could be surface patches or NURBS (Non-Uniform Rational B-Splines), or CSG (Constructive Solid Geometry).
- The model may contain too many polygons.
- The model may contain polygons, when the VR system supports triangles.
- The vertex sequence of polygons may be different to that used in the VR system.
- The vertex sequence of polygons may not be consistent.
- The model may include duplicate polygons.
- The strategy for handling texture maps may be different.

There are many more such problems that have to be resolved by the filtering software.

Libraries

Most VR software systems provide a 3D library of some sort; this may be in the form of a collection of simple primitives such as polygons, boxes, spheres, cones, pyramids, etc., that can be assembled to create equally primitive VEs. Likewise, other libraries provide complete VEs in the form of office and home furniture, everyday objects, and complete rooms and offices. These are useful as they provide a starting point to become accustomed with working with a VE.

Level of detail

Level Of Detail (LOD) is a system feature for optimizing the amount of detail rendered in a scene. For example, a model of a virtual house will require a lot of detail when viewed close to: it will include windows, doors, a chimney, gutters, and even individual tiles and bricks. If we go inside the house we could find internal walls, doors, stairs, furniture, and every type of fixture and fitting. However, if we look at the house from a distance of 500 m, individual tiles and bricks will appear very small, and we will certainly not be able to discern any internal contents through the windows. If we move even further away, some of the external features will disappear completely. Obviously, it would be a waste of time to render the same virtual model at these different distances:

what is required are different models with appropriate levels of detail. A model viewed close up will contain fine levels of geometric detail, but when viewed at a great distance another model is substituted with corresponding lower levels of detail.

A LOD strategy requires copies of important models to be built that will be rendered at user defined distances. These are stored together in the VE database, and the relevant model is rendered at the appropriate distance. This takes up extra disk space and memory at run time, but the rendering time saved makes it worthwhile.

One of the drawbacks of the technique is that it can be obvious when a model substitution is made. At one moment we see a view of a house, for example, with a particular LOD, and then all of a sudden a new one is substituted. The human visual system is particularly efficient at noticing such changes. However, the impact of the substitution can be minimized by fading out one view of the model and fading in the second view over a given distance and time. But this does require the renderer to handle transparency.

Another form of LOD control can be used when very large databases are manipulated, and cannot be rendered in real time. When the view is stationary the user sees the highest level of detail possible. But as soon as the user navigates through the database the LOD switches to an appropriate level that permits a specific update rate to be maintained. When navigation stops, the database returns to its highest LOD.

Very powerful automatic software tools are available to create the alternative LODs of the database, and are generally prepared off line. This LOD strategy is particularly useful when manipulating very large CAD files.

Object scaling, rotating and translating

Some VR models may be nothing more than an imported CAD model, and will require very little manipulation. On the other hand, some VEs may require careful construction from several dozen individual elements. In the case of a house, the internal and external walls, windows, chimney and roof will probably be modeled as one unit. Other features, such as doors, shelves, stairs, lights, work surfaces, cupboards, etc., will be modeled and installed individually.

To begin with, everything must share a common scale. Remember that a virtual house does not have to have coordinates that match a real house; coordinates do not have any physical units—they are pure numeric quantities. Maintaining a common scale is very easy—one simply multiplies or divides the object's coordinates by an appropriate number. In the jargon of computer graphics this operation is called a *scaling transform*.

An object may have to be rotated before it is finally positioned, and various tools must be available to rotate specified angles about different axes. For instance, a ladder may have been modeled in a vertical position, but its place in the VE is leaning against a wall. Similarly, a door may be modeled facing the front of the house, and will have to be rotated by appropriate angles if it is to used in all of the rooms. Object rotation is achieved by a *rotation transform*.

Finally, once an object has been scaled and rotated, it has to be located within the VE using a *translation transform*. The use of these three transforms is a common procedure in VR software but the user rarely has to use them directly. Object scaling, rotating and translating are normally effected through a GUI (Graphics User Interface) which makes life very easy. Fig. 6.1 illustrates what happens to a box when it is subjected to a scale, translate and rotate transform.

But if VR is so good at interacting with 3D worlds, why not use a VR system to build a VE? Well, this can be done using MultiGen's Creator product.

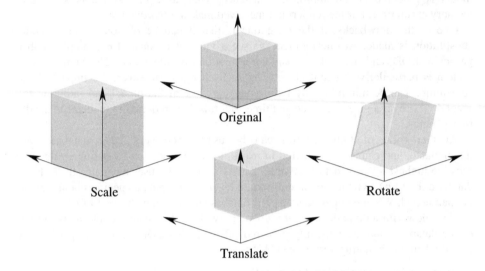

Fig. 6.1 *The effects of scaling, translating and rotating an object.*

Constraints

As we have already discovered, certain virtual objects require constraining to make them behave like their real world counterparts. For example, a door requires to be constrained by its hinges and frame; a draw needs to slide in and out; the side windows of a car have to slide up and down; a light switch must turn on and off, and a tap must turn clockwise and anti-clockwise. Such constraint information requires specifying and stored within the VE database. Thus when a VR user interacts with these objects, the database determines the limits of travel and prevents inconsistent manipulation. For instance, we would not want to approach a virtual door, request it to open, and find that it became attached to our hand! What we do want, is for the door to open and be pushed to its physical limit without rotating through the supporting wall.

Other types of constraint include forcing objects to follow the floor height and preventing objects from intersecting other objects.

Articulated features

VR is a very powerful tool for visualizing CAD models that often includes interconnecting elements. In the case of a car, for example, when one turns a real steering wheel, the front wheels turn accordingly; but one could not expect this to happen at a virtual level without a lot of work. It just so happens that such articulated features can be incorporated by identifying linked elements in a virtual object and forcing them to move whenever other elements move. Thus a VR user could use the controls of a virtual earth-moving vehicle to operate its hydraulically controlled digger. See Plate 10. Such a facility is very useful for exploring the operational envelope of a piece of machinery and evaluating all sorts of ergonomic issues.

Animation

We have seen that it is possible to simulate the physical connectivity between various elements, which requires some preprocessing of the database and extra processing at run time. However, it is not always necessary to simulate movements with such accuracy, and one can introduce simple animation to create a variety of animated behaviors. In flight simulation animated models are used to mimic the behavior of virtual ground crew assisting in bringing the virtual plane into a docking position. A sequence of models can be stored in the database in different positions, and can be played back in real time to create an animated effect. Although this requires extra effort to build the various models, it saves the processing time that would have been used to transform a single model into different positions.

Animation techniques can be used to simulate doors opening, water flowing, wheels rotating, weather effects, explosions, etc. Even video clips can be introduced into a VE by playing back MPEG files as an animated texture map.

Plates 14 and 15 show two views of Venice modeled using Superscape's VRT system. As one navigates about the model in a gondola, the water moves up and down with a wave-like motion. This is achieved by storing approximately 30 copies of the water in the form of a triangular mesh. Each copy of the mesh is then distorted to simulate an undulating wave motion, such that when played back as an animation, the water appears to move up and down.

Collision detection

We already know that collision detection provides a method for selecting objects within a VE. For example, when a hand-held 3D mouse is used to guide the virtual cursor inside a VE, the polygons associated with the cursor can be tested for collision against other objects. When a collision is detected, we can request that the object be associated with the cursor, which can be used to reposition the object. It is the real-time software environment that undertakes this task, and because collision detection can become very time consuming, especially when one complex object is compared with the VE, very efficient algorithms are essential.

In order to keep the VR system running as fast as possible collision detection must be kept to a minimum, but there are many occasions when it provides the only way of working. Thus a user will require to activate and deactivate this mode of working even when working immersively, which calls for appropriate interface tools.

Parallel worlds

The rather imposing name of *parallel worlds* has been borrowed from the esoteric regions of cosmology, but in this context it simply means multiple databases. One can move from one world (VE database) to another by passing through a portal which is a doorway connecting to another VE. It is a convenient way of moving from the outside of a building into its inside without having to store one large database. When outside the building we cannot see its inside and *vice versa*. Whenever we pass through the portal the real-time software makes the necessary database substitution.

Light sources

At some stage lights have to be positioned within the VE. This may be nothing more than setting an ambient level and one major light source. However, if the VE is representing a detailed interior model, and illumination levels are important, several lights will have to be positioned and adjusted to create the required effect.

Perhaps the most sophisticated lighting model is radiosity that simulates inter-reflections, color bleeding and soft shadows. Although there is no real-time solution at the moment, it is possible to compute these light levels off line and import them integral with the VE geometry. This creates highly realistic images with hardly any run-time overhead. Because shadows and illumination are integral with the geometry, their values cannot be changed on line. Plates 5 and 6 show excellent examples of the radiosity technique.

Event handling

Specific actions or animation are called *events* and require software to ensure they are correctly activated. Such events may take the form of doors opening automatically, an object reaching some destination, or the user moving into a special zone in the VE. For example, a virtual airplane attempting to land can have its landing gear automatically brought down when it reaches a set height above ground. Similarly, a VR user undergoing training using a VE could wander into a 'dangerous' area and trigger an event in the form of a MPEG video clip. Whatever the reason, events can be activated to add that extra level of realism to a VE.

Audio

The VR software system must also control the playback of sound files associated with different objects and zones of a VE. Such sounds include ticking clocks, running engines, radios, telephones, machinery, human voices, and all sorts of ambient background noises. The sound volume, as heard by the VR user, can also be modulated by the user's distance from the object. And a virtual radio, for example, could be switched on by touching its virtual on/off switch, or the engine noise of a mechanical digger could become louder every time it undertook a heavy task.

Where required, the VR software must also support 3D sound systems.

Control language

Just as a scripting language is needed in certain computer animation software systems, a similar control language is required to animate objects within a VE. For example, in a VR training exercise, when a user performs a certain action, a script is executed that undertakes a set task. This could be anything from a opening a door to animating a bottling plant when a button is pushed. Either way, the script is interpreted by the real-time software to activate a preset animation.

Simulation

In the early days of VR the general public imagined that a virtual world was similar to the real world. How wrong they were! Very little happens inside a VE unless it is programmed, and if anything makes it happen, it is software.

Simulation software is complex and even the simplest of activities requires intense programming. Take, for example, object collision. When two real objects collide they obey Newtonian mechanics, which states that the momentum of the two objects remains constant before and after the impact. The momentum is the product of the object's mass and velocity. This is easy to compute mathematically, but when two irregular objects collide, their impact can give rise to an infinite number of collision scenarios that cannot be predicted. If accuracy is required the mathematical solution requires knowledge of the object's masses, linear velocities, angular velocities, moments of inertia, surface attributes, gravity, etc. But even then, it will be only possible to compute an approximate simulation if the answer is required in real time.

Therefore, unless there is a limited role for simulation within a typical VR system, substantial levels of processing power are available to execute the simulation programs. However, current software is attempting to simulate the effects of mass, gravitational forces, and forces due to interaction and collisions. With appropriate hardware such forces can be returned to the user via joysticks, gloves and articulated arms.

Sensors

Anyone who has attempted to interface the simplest of devices to a computer will know of the technical challenge it presents. Not only is it necessary to have a detailed knowledge of the device, but it is essential to have an intimate knowledge of the host operating system, whether it be Windows, Windows NT or UNIX. For devices such as printers, scanners, modems, fax machines, etc., there are some very efficient software tools for installing these in a matter of minutes, but the installation of HMDs, trackers, 3D mice, etc., requires careful handling.

VR software must include appropriate tools to interface the various sensors, and enable them to work within a real-time environment. Fortunately, this is an area that has been addressed by the VR community.

Stereo viewing

Although HMDs have left and right screens to operate stereoscopically, it can be arranged for them to work monoscopically where both eyes see the same image. It is also necessary to adjust, at a software level, the distance between the user's virtual eyes (the inter-pupilary distance), and the degree of overlap between the left and right images. Some systems are also able to provide a parallel as well as a perspective projection of the VE.

Tracking

Tracking technology is a vital feature of any VR system and several systems are commercially available. Software support is required to enable the tracker's position to be located within the VE and adjusted to give the user a useful point of view.

Networking

Some VR systems can be networked together so that two distant users can share a common VE and interact collaboratively. Under such conditions there has to be a fast exchange of information between the computers.

Let us examine the case of two users: User-A and User-B who have the same VE installed in their computers. User-A will want to see User-B in his/her HMD, and *vice versa*, therefore the position of the two users must be exchanged. This enables each host computer to display a 3D mannequin of the other user. Such a mannequin is called an *avatar*. Each user's hand position must also be exchanged so that the avatar's arm and hand can be animated. Finally, the name of the object selected, together with its position and orientation must be exchanged, so that each computer can display the final scene.

By exchanging this minimal level of data over a fast communication network, two users can see each other at a virtual level and interact with a single object. However, only one user can have control of an object at any one time, but if each user takes it in turns, software will look after the transfer of control.

Plate 11 shows two avatars handling a component within a shared VE.

Web based VR

Introduction to VRML

Users of the World Wide Web (WWW) will be aware of its ability to distribute text and images across the network, but in recent years great strides have been made in implementing a strategy for distributing 3D worlds. The HTML (Hyper-Text Markup Language) has become the *de facto* standard for describing documents with hyper-links, and a similar language was required for supporting interactive simulation within the WWW. The Virtual Reality Modeling Language (VRML) is the result—although it initially started its life as the Virtual Reality Markup Language.

In 1994 the first WWW Conference was held in Geneva, Switzerland, and Tim Berners-Lee and Dave Raggett led a group to discuss the requirements of a 3D graphical language. It had to be platform independent, extensible and work over low-bandwidth networks. It was also decided that the first version of VRML would not support interactive behaviors—this would have to wait for a later revision.

The idea of attempting to implement 3D graphics over the Internet still seems a strange idea, especially when the system response of the Web can appear as though the whole world is connected, to one being the only user! But VRML has proved to be a great success.

Fortunately, it was not necessary to start from scratch, as it was possible to call upon an extensive history of 3D computer graphics. And in the end, Silicon Graphics' Open Inventor ASCII file format became the basis of VRML as it already supported polygonal objects, lighting, materials, rendering and texture mapping.

VRML Browsers

A VRML file stores a description of a 3D world in the form of graphic primitives, their color and texture, and how they are to be viewed by a virtual camera. It is also possible to subject the objects to the transforms: scale, translate and rotate. When such a file is stored on the Web, any user can download it and store it on their computer. Then with the aid of a suitable browser, such as Netscape's Navigator with a Cosmo Player plug-in, it is possible to convert the ASCII file into a 3D image. But as the browser is equipped with tools to rotate, pan and track, one can navigate a 3D model in real time. It's the speed of the host computer that determines the processing speed, rather than the communication network.

VRML 1.0 specification

Although this is not the place to give a complete overview of VRML, it is worth exploring some of its features in order to appreciate its potential. A full specification is located at http://www.vrml.org/VRML1.0/vrml10c.html.

Nodes

Nodes are the building blocks for creating 3D computer graphics, and include cubes, spheres, cones, cylinders, etc.; transformations (scale, translate and rotate), colors, textures, viewing perspective, etc. The nodes are organized into a specific sequence called a *scene graph* such that when they are traversed, their order determines the sequence the 3D world is created.

A node can also influence other nodes further along the scene graph. For example, a color node can be declared such that any following object nodes can be given the same color. Similarly, a scaling transform node could be used to collectively translate a number of object nodes. In order to cancel the influence of these nodes a *separator node* is used to partition the scene graph into organized structures.

A node has the following characteristics:

- **Object type** (cube, sphere, texture map, transform, viewer orientation, etc).
- **Node parameters** (height, radius, width, depth, red, green, blue, x, y, z, etc.).
- **Name of node** (an arbitrary name to allow multiple referencing).
- **Child nodes** (nodes that belong to a larger hierarchy).

VRML file format

The first line of a VRML 2.0 file must contain the characters "#VRML V2.0 <text>". Subsequent lines refer to the nodes that comprise the scene graph. As internal documentation is a *must* for all computer languages, VRML employs the "#" symbol to delineate the start of a comment, and is terminated by a new line.

The rest of the file comprise a number of statements about the position of the camera, texture maps, the type of object, the object's position, etc. For example, the geometry for a cube could be defined as:

geometry Cube {height 4 width 3 depth 2}

and a sphere as:

geometry Sphere {radius 2}

The default position for a perspective camera is ($x = 0$, $y = 0$, $z = 1$) but this can be overridden by the following command:

PerspectiveCamera {position 0 1 20}

Every other command has its own list of parameters. A complete VRML1.0 program is shown in Appendix D.

The first version of VRML was issued about 5 years ago, and since then version 2.0 has surfaced with many more extras. In December 1997, VRML97 replaced VRML 2.0 and was formally released as International Standard ISO/IEC 14772. If you really want to find out more about VRML 2.0, take a look at Jed Hartman and Josie Wernecke's book *The VRML 2.0 Handbook* (Hartman and Wernecke, 1996).

The following VRML program produces the image in Fig. 6.2. But by using the interactive tools in the browser one can immediately rotate the scene to obtain the view shown in Fig. 6.3.

```
#VRML V2.0 utf8
Background {skyColor 1.0 1.0 1.0}
Group {
 children [
  # Box shape
  Shape {
    appearance Appearance {
      material Material {
        diffuseColor 1.0 1.0 0.0}
    }
   geometry Box { size 3.0 3.0 3.0}
  }
  # Sphere shape
  Shape {
    appearance Appearance {
      material Material {
        diffuseColor 0.0 1.0 0.0}
    }
   geometry Sphere {radius 1.8}
  }
  # Right Sphere
  Transform { translation 5.0 0.0 0.0
    children [
      Shape { appearance Appearance {
        material Material {
          diffuseColor 0.9 0.9 1.0}
      }
      geometry Sphere {radius 2.5}
    }
   ]
  }
 }
 # Left Sphere
```

```
Transform { translation -4.0 0.0 0.0
  children [
  Shape {
    appearance Appearance {
      material Material {
        diffuseColor 0.8 0.8 0.5}
    }
    geometry Cone { bottomRadius 2.0 height 4.0
                    side TRUE bottom TRUE}
  }
 ]
 }
]
}
```

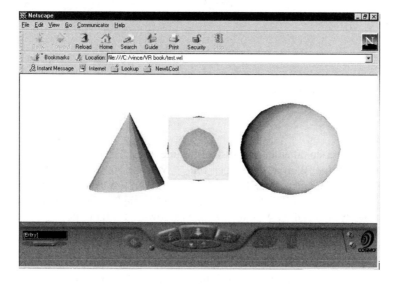

Fig. 6.2 *Output of the above VRML program.*

As one can see, even small programs are very verbose, and large programs require great care to assemble. Fortunately, a variety of interactive software tools are available to ease the design of VRML worlds. One such product is Superscape's 3D Webmaster. It provides a simple 3D, modeling environment, runs on a PC and integrates the geometry with HTML, Java and JavaScript. However, the product that is really appropriate to VR is Superscape's VRT.

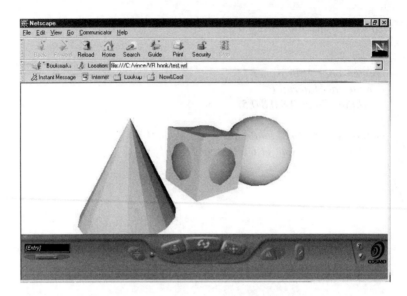

Fig. 6.3 Rotated view of VRML model.

Superscape's VRT

VRT Overview

VRT 5.5 is a professional authoring system for interactive 3D worlds on a PC. They can be published on the Web using Superscape's Viscape, or used by Visualiser in a standalone mode. The recommended hardware configuration is a Pentium II processor, 64 MB of RAM, 1 GB hard disk, SVGA 1280 x 1024 graphics card, and a Spacemouse. The operating system can be Windows 95 or Windows NT 4.0 or later.

VRT divides into three sections: authoring, browsing and content. Authoring provides seven editors that let you create interactive VEs using a 'drag-and-drop' interface. 3D objects with behaviors, textures and sound can be modeled using the Shape Editor, Image Editor and Sound Editor. Object behaviors, dynamics, and angular velocity between objects, can be copied-and-pasted using internal libraries, or written using the internal SCL (Superscape Scripting Language) scripting language.

The browsing section enables a world to be previewed as it is being developed, and the content section consists of large libraries of Virtual Clip Art objects, textures, and sounds that make it easy and quick to build 3D worlds. For example, one can add a piano that plays; clocks that tell the time; and animated people who can occupy a world and avoid collisions. In all, VRT contains 800 Virtual Clip Art objects, 500 textures, and 200 sounds.

Devices

VRT supports a wide range of graphics cards, input devices, and sound cards. The default installation, however, assumes that only the mouse, keyboard and SVGA graphics card are connected to the VRT system. If additional devices are needed an interactive setup process allows various drivers to be enabled.

Proportional devices

VRT supports a variety of proportional devices such as joysticks, the Logitech Spacemouse, Spaceball Technologies' Spaceball, Ascension Flock of Birds motion tracker, Polhemus FASTRAK motion tracker and Virtual I-O i-glasses. All of these devices can be configured to alter their sensitivity and spatial conventions.

File formats

The data for each world is held by VRT in an uncompressed binary data .VRT file. However, when a new world is constructed it is saved as a .SVR file for display in Viscape, or a .XVR file for display in Visualiser, which are compressed file formats. The compressed format is particularly suitable for the Web, and minimizes download time.

In addition to handling files in VRT format, the World Editor can import and export files in VRML 2.0 format using a .WRL extension. The Image editor imports and exports files in any of the following formats:

- .PCX   A common computer graphics file format that is supported by most graphics applications.
- .BMP   A Windows bitmap that is supported by many applications.
- .GIF   A CompuServe graphics format that uses the LZW compression standard.
- .JPG   A graphics format that uses the JPEG compression standard. JPEG uses a 'lossy' algorithm—where some of the sharpness in the image is lost in the compression process.
- .TIF   A TIFF image handles monochrome, grayscale and color images.
- .TGA   A Targa graphics file format that supports true color high definition images.

VRT lets you import standard Windows .WAV files into the Sound Editor in uncompressed PCM format or Ad Lib .SMP files. VRT only plays mono sounds, so if stereo sounds are imported, only one channel can be input. However, one can use VRT's Autosounds or SCL to create a stereo effect.

Visualiser and Viscape

Visualiser and Viscape let you display, move around, and interact with the worlds that you create in the editors. You can adjust display options, viewpoints, and device configurations, to add the final touches to a world. You can switch from the editors to Visualiser or Viscape at any time to see the changes that you have made, such as altering a shape, object, SCL program, or system configuration.

World Editor

World Editor is used to build worlds from preconstructed objects known as Virtual Clip Art (VCA), or objects whose profile is defined by the Shape Editor. Completed objects are then placed individually, or grouped together, resized and colored in the new world.

Further attributes can be added in the form of texture, sound, dynamics, animation, lighting, distancing (LOD) and behaviors.

Whilst this world building is in progress it is possible to move around the objects and view them from any viewpoint using a mouse, keyboard or proportional device.

Building blocks

VRT worlds consist of simple orthogonal objects like building blocks. Each object can range in complexity from a single point in space to an animated object that is fully controllable with built-in intelligence.

Bounding cubes

Every object and shape in the world is placed within its own bounding cube, an invisible cube that defines the space the object occupies in a world. VRT uses bounding cubes to order objects and shapes correctly in the world; and if an object rotates in the world, the bounding cube also rotates.

Points, facets, shapes and objects

The smallest building block in VRT is a 3D point, and is used to construct facets, shapes and objects.

Facets are 1D (a line) or 2D surfaces created by connecting two or more points together. They have a front but no back—the front is colored and the reverse is invisible. When the normal single sided facet is facing away from the viewpoint, it cannot be seen, and is ignored by VRT.

Facets are created in the Shape Editor, and are grouped together to create shapes which define the profile of objects in the world. All the facets in a shape are listed in a facet list that VRT uses to render the shape.

A shape consists of the combined facet and point information contained inside a bounding cube. They can be made of flat facets, or smooth-shaded to create more realistic objects.

An object is simply any item in the world, which has been built in the World Editor from the shapes. They can be very simple, such as a cube, or very complex with a range of attributes.

To simplify world descriptions you can construct complex objects as a single 'group' object, and then treat all the objects as a single object. Grouping objects together, not only makes it easier to create complex objects, but also increases the speed at which VRT can draw the world. Groups can have exactly the same range of attributes as simple objects. Fig. 6.4 shows how a table is made from a group of individual objects.

Attributes

Attributes are key features that can be attached to an object or group in the World editor to specify unique properties. Each object has a set of standard attributes—such as size, position, shape—and additional attributes like textures, sounds, motion, behaviors and URLs. You can change the attributes of a single object without affecting any other aspect of the object or group.

Fig. 6.4 *Modeling a table from a group of objects.*
(Image courtesy of Superscape).

Dynamic objects

Shapes and objects can be given a wide range of dynamic features to match the dynamics of objects in the real world. These include gravity, climbing, falling, friction, restitution, driving velocity, external velocity and maximum velocity.

- **Gravity**: the object accelerates under a gravitational force by altering the object's vertical velocity at a rate of g per frame downwards (where g is the acceleration due to gravity 9.81 m/sec/sec), towards the ground (Y=0 plane).

- **Climbing**: the object can climb or fall over objects in its path depending on the values given it—for example, a virtual human must have a climbing attribute to go up stairs and gravity to go down stairs.

- **Falling**: defines the maximum drop an object can make when climbing down from an obstacle without it being damaged. If it falls by a distance greater than that specified by the falling value, it is stopped and flagged as having fallen 'too far'.

- **Friction**: slows down a moving object according to the value given to it. In VRT, friction is applied to each moving object rather than the surface over which objects move. For example, applying a friction attribute of 10% to an object would slow its external velocity by 1/10 from frame to frame, until the object's external velocity is reduced to such a low value that it appears to come to a halt.

- **Restitution**: changes an object's velocity after a collision. When an object hits a surface, the object's external velocity is multiplied by the restitution, and the direction of the velocity is reversed. For example, if a ball is given a vertical restitution value of 75% and it hits the floor at a downward velocity of 100, it bounces up with an upward velocity of 75.

- **Driving velocity**: sets the velocity at which an object moves under its own power, independent of any other force in the world—this velocity is constant and unaltered by friction, but is affected by the rotation of the object to which movement is coupled.

- **External velocity**: sets the external velocity of an object—this is normally set by the system, and is affected by friction.
- **Maximum velocity**: sets the maximum driving velocity of an object—it has no effect on the external velocity of an object.

The human figure in Fig. 6.5 is able to walk up or down a flight of stairs because it has been endowed with climbing, gravity and falling.

Fig. 6.5 *Figure walking downstairs under the action of gravity.*
(Image courtesy of Superscape)

Animations

To change one shape into another, the two shapes are supplied to VRT, which automatically creates all of the in-between shapes needed for the animation sequence.

The visualization system

In order to maximize image fidelity and rendering speed, VRT's visualization system offers the following features.

Bounding cubes and volumes

A *bounding cube*, whose size can be adjusted so that it matches the object as closely as possible, defines the orthogonal space an object occupies in a world.

Objects also have a volume that VRT uses to check for collisions between objects. An object's *volume* is the orthogonal space an object occupies within the default axes. If the object has dynamics or rotations, its volume may be different to its bounding cube as it must cover all the possible positions of the object's components, otherwise it is the same as the bounding cube.

Sorting and rendering

VRT renders each frame using a combination of object sorting and Z-buffering, and the user can select the level according to the complexity of the world. VRT first works out where objects are positioned relative to the current viewpoint. It then draws the object furthest away, overlaying the other objects until it has drawn the nearest last. If VRT detects objects that may cause a drawing problem it automatically Z-buffers them as it renders the frame. VRT also draws the facets in each shape in the order defined by its facet list, unless it decides to Z-buffer the object.

Z-buffering can be set from none to full buffering. If you want to draw your world using object sorting solely (which is generally the fastest method), you can use various association techniques to group the facets and objects, so that VRT does not have to draw all the facets and objects.

Distancing

As an object recedes into the distance, you can replace it with a simpler one that takes less time to process, since the detail on its facets become more difficult for the human eye to differentiate. A distancing attribute specifies the distance from the viewpoint at which an object is replaced by a simpler object, and the object that replaces it. This replacement can be repeated as many times as necessary for each object, until it disappears from sight. Fig. 6.6 shows two figures modeled at two LODs.

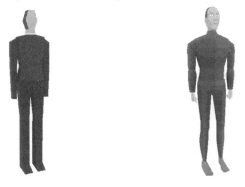

***Fig. 6.6** A human figure modeled at two levels of detail.*
(Image courtesy of Superscape)

Color

VRT decides the color it uses for each object from a palette of 256 colors, the screen depth and the graphics mode in use. If lighting is on in the world, VRT takes the base color of each facet from the palette and then adjusts it to use the screen depth being used, in order to create smooth-shaded objects. If lighting is off, VRT just uses the base color from the palette.

Textures

Textures can be used to increase the level of realism of the world. They can be mapped to objects in various ways, such as single facets or all the facets in a color range, or to create special effects such as cylinders and spheres. Plates 14 and 15 show two views of virtual Venice modeled in VRT running on a PC. The textures are reflected in the water by building a duplicate model upside-down, and a cycle of approximately 30 surface states animates the water.

Lighting

VRT allows ten active light sources in a world. It calculates the amount of light from each source falling on objects, and uses this to color them in real time.

Light sources can be attached to objects, so that they move and rotate with the object. They can be dimmed, turned on and off, and their beam characteristics altered using Superscape's Control Language SCL. Processing time can be saved and the update rate increased by making the lighting calculation once when the world is loaded or reset. This is particularly suitable for static worlds.

Fog

VRT can support different atmospheric conditions, such as night scenes and smoky interiors, using fog and the background. In general, a distance is set at which visibility in the world starts to fade, and a distance at which objects become invisible. Fig. 6.7 shows two views of a ship with fog switched off and on. Plate 14 also shows some mist in the background scene of Venice.

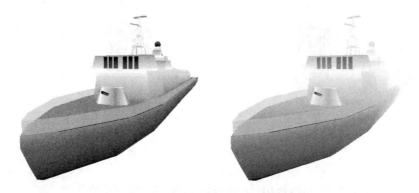

Fig. 6.7 *Switching fog on and off.*
(Image courtesy of Superscape)

Sound

Sounds can be attached to objects to enhance the realism of worlds, which can be triggered automatically or played by a simple SCL program. For example, sounds can include background noises, or instructions to the user. Sounds can be made louder or quieter as you move in and out or the world, and create directional sounds.

VRT Summary

It is easy to see that the designers of Superscape's VRT system had a deep insight into the needs of people creating 3D worlds. The product is extremely easy to use and the 'drag-and-drop' interface makes world building easier than typing. In fact, I was amazed to see how easy it was to create a sample office in a matter of seconds and drop animated humans who would avoid each other as well as the office furniture!

VRT is widely used in industry to implement a wide variety of 3D worlds that are used in all sorts of applications from marketing to training, and I will return to such applications in the next chapter.

Division's dVISE

Overview of dVISE

Division Ltd. has pioneered the design of VR software to meet the demanding needs of the industrial sector. Their dVISE system is the result of many years' R&D effort and collaborative industrial projects that have given VR a true professional image.

dVISE allows a designer to create a virtual representation of a product (i.e. a virtual product) based upon the engineering data from a CAD database. It allows the designer to add audio, visual, and behavioral characteristics (such as animation, movement constraints, and collision properties) to this representation, so that dVISE can model the interaction of the product's component parts and the interaction of the product with human operators.

dVISE is a modular product with each module carefully targeting a specific function. All modules support SGI, HP, and Sun UNIX platforms in addition to PCs running Windows NT. A summary of all the modules is included in the following sub-sections and listed in order of increasing functionality.

All dVISE modules support interactive navigation through the virtual product using a normal desktop mouse and workstation monitor. Some modules support more advanced peripherals, such as 3D mice and stereo head-mounted displays. In addition, many modules include advanced navigation aids that allow users to fly to stored positions via an iconic graphical user interface.

dV/WebFly

The dV/WebFly module allows virtual products to be published on the Internet and viewed using a freely available plug-in for commercial HTML browsers. In the wider community the plug-in modules for commercial HTML browsers are freely available from Division.

dV/Player

The dV/Player module is a high performance visualization tool. It is designed for real-time navigation of very large assemblies and provides users with the capability to move assemblies, to view Landmarks (camera views), and to playback complex animations. This module includes a basic level of collision detection in which a bounding box represents each assembly.

Output from this module is displayed on a workstation, with support for CrystalEyes glasses for a pseudo stereo effect. Navigation is controlled by a conventional mouse, a Spaceball, or a Spacemouse.

dV/Review

The dV/Review module includes all the functionality of the dV/Player module, but also allows the user to create, edit, and view Landmarks (camera views) and user Annotations (user notes), and to save these definitions to the file system as part of the virtual product's definition. The Virtual Product Manager is included in this module, and may be used to view and edit the assembly hierarchy (using a 2D graphical display), to selectively load or unload assemblies, and to send dVISE events to assemblies.

dV/MockUp

The dV/MockUp module includes all the functionality of the dV/Review module, plus fast polygonal collision detection, interference analysis, and extended Virtual Product Manager capabilities. The latter allows the user to edit the assembly structure, to define the animation properties of assemblies, to add user data into the assembly hierarchy, and to define the illumination of the virtual product.

The fast polygonal collision detection algorithms enable the user to study the interaction of complex assemblies in real time, and are ideally suited to the modeling of assembly/disassembly sequences. dV/MockUp and dV/Reality are the only modules that include this feature; other modules use fast bounding box collision detection in which the collision boundaries of each assembly are modeled by a bounding box.

Users of dV/MockUp and dV/Reality may perform a product-wide interference analysis on the virtual product to check that assemblies do not interfere or overlap by more than a specified tolerance. The interference test may take the form of a single query or it may accommodate animated models via a continuous query and real-time display of results. In either case an interference report identifies assembly pairs that were found to collide and the points of collision. Optional links between the Interference Manager and the dVISE View allows the affected assemblies to be brought into view and highlighted.

The Virtual Product Manager functionality that is provided by dV/MockUp allows you to add assemblies into a hierarchy that defines a virtual product. You can associate user data with each assembly, perhaps recording the source of the data or general design notes. You can also edit and view the position, visual, and collision properties of the assemblies to specify their appearance and the way they respond to manipulation.

dV/Reality

The dV/Reality modules includes all the capabilities of the dV/MockUp module, but extends the functionality of the Virtual Product Manager allowing you to design a fully functional model of your virtual product.

With the dV/Reality module you can specify the behavior of your assemblies (i.e. how they respond to events) allowing you to model the way that your assemblies interact and respond to external influences. You can also constrain movements, and you can associate audio properties (such as musical or special effect sounds). You can also link assemblies to create assembly hierarchies that operate as a single entity; movement (or any other manipulation) of one entity will then affect those that are linked to it.

With the dV/Reality module you can define a fully functional virtual prototype that can be viewed by any of the dVISE modules.

Common components

The dV/Geometry Tools component is an integral part of all the dV/Review, dV/MockUp, and dV/Reality modules. It includes stand-alone (off-line) converters and geometry processing tools for AutoDesk 3D Studio, DXF, Alias/Wavefront, and Multigen formats. A number of options are also available for importing engineering data from specialist CAD environments. Currently supported formats include: EDS Unigraphics, Pro/Engineer, Computervision CADDS and Optegra, IBM/Dassault CATIA, Bentley MicroStation and Intergraph (IGDS), Inventor, and IGES.

The dV/Collaboration component adds a networked multi-user capability to the dV/Review, dV/MockUp, and dV/Reality modules (and is available as an option for the dV/Player module). It also allows many users to view and interact with the virtual product concurrently and via a corporate local or wide area network.

Optional components

dV/Manikin: This option adds human modeling to all of the dVISE modules. It allows you to simulate the interaction between your virtual product and its human operators for applications such as ergonomics and component accessibility.

dV/Immersion: This option adds a full immersive capability to all dVISE modules, and allows the use of 3D peripherals such as head-mounted displays and 3D mice.

dV/ITools: This option adds an immersive ToolBox, allowing you to control and define the VE immersively.

dV/Developer: This option provides libraries and header files that let C programmers extend the capabilities of dVISE by defining new actions functions and new tools for an immersive ToolBox. You can also build upon Division's low-level interface to develop a custom application that replaces dVISE and more closely models the requirements of your virtual products.

A virtual product

Division defines a virtual product as one or more assemblies that are typically derived from CAD environments, and are converted into a form that is suitable for rendering by using the dVISE Geometry Tools.

During the conversion process the Geometry Tools extract from the CAD database all data that is relevant to interactive visualization. This includes the logical structure of assemblies (i.e. the sub-assembly hierarchy), color and layer partitioning, assembly names, materials and textures, user defined annotations, and, of course, the geometric data. After the conversion process the assemblies are represented by an assembly or product structure file that records the overall structure of the product, and by binary files that represent the geometric and material data.

VDI files

The VDI file is the top-level representation of an assembly. It is a human readable (ASCII) scripting language for defining virtual products. Within it you can define many assemblies and assembly hierarchies, their interdependencies, and their properties.

Each CAD conversion generates a single top-level VDI file representing an assembly or assembly hierarchy. Many conversions can be performed, possibly converting data from many different CAD environments, each resulting in a VDI file representation. dVISE allows the designer to assemble these VDI files into a product structure, and to assign physical properties that describe their interaction. The resulting product can be saved to a new VDI file that records the full product definition.

The dVISE geometry tools

The interface to the dVISE Geometry Tools is via a simple graphical user interface. At the simplest level the tools will convert the geometric data into a form that is suitable for rendering (i.e. tessellation), and will also perform optimization, welding, reduction and other geometric functions to maximize image quality and rendering performance.

Some high-end CAD environments also support active links with dVISE, and allow the export and conversion of data from within the CAD environment.

A key capability of the geometry tools is the ability to generate appropriate Levels Of Detail (LODs). As a user moves around in the VE, dVISE optionally selects the most appropriate LOD to maximize image quality while retaining acceptable navigation performance. When the user stops moving the assemblies that are close to the viewpoint are switched to a high resolution form that allows detailed analysis.

Interacting with the virtual product

You can view a virtual product on a conventional computer display within a dedicated window, called the dVISE View that can be resized and moved anywhere on the screen. You interact with the virtual product by using a conventional computer mouse, or a Spaceball or Spacemouse that provide a more intuitive way to manipulate the product in three dimensions. CrystalEyes glasses allow you to generate pseudo stereo displays from a workstation's monoscopic display.

For the greatest control you can use a stereo head-mounted display and a 3D mouse, which allow you to immerse yourself in a VE, and to move around and interact with the product in the most natural and productive way.

dVISE navigation aids

Some dVISE modules build upon the explicit directional controls of the hardware devices to provide a number of higher-level software controls. You access these controls via the Virtual Product Manager which provides the user interface to all the high level navigation and design capabilities of dVISE.

Navigator view

The Navigator View allows you to control your position in the VE by entering explicit directional or rotational movements into a graphical user interface. This achieves more accurate positioning than the hardware controls, particularly for small incremental movements. See Fig. 6.8.

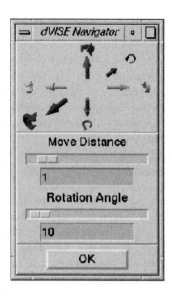

Fig. 6.8 *Navigator's controls.*
(Image courtesy of Division)

Cameras, flight paths, and landmarks

A user can place cameras at interesting points in the assembly hierarchy to record important views of the assemblies. You can see these cameras represented as icons in the Assembly Manager, but the Landmark Browser provides a more intuitive (and more widely available) interface.

Flight paths build on the functionality of cameras to define an animated view of the virtual product. As with cameras there is an iconic representation of flight paths in the Assembly Manager, and links may be created from the Landmark Browser. When you activate a flight path or camera, your virtual body is flown smoothly along a prescribed path producing an animated view of the product.

Annotations

The Annotation Browser allows designers and reviewers to attach text messages (optionally with audio, visual, and behavioral properties) to a view, and to send the textual message of the annotation to other members of their team via a corporate e-mail system. The Annotation Browser collates the annotations and their responses into a graphical 2D display. When you review an annotation you can playback its associated voice recording and fly-to the appropriate assemblies in the virtual environment. The annotation may also define actions that bring the virtual product (or parts of it) to life.

Events and actions

All dVISE modules support an event/action paradigm that allows complex behavior to be modeled. A designer can define the events that an assembly responds to and the list of actions that are to be performed in response to those events. For example, an assembly might move or play an audio track when it is touched. The events may be issued by dVISE in response to physical stimuli (for example, when you touch an assembly) but more commonly they are issued by other assemblies to model their interaction.

Multiple users and roles

Most dVISE modules support a collaboration option that allows users to work together within a VE. Users connect to dVISE from their own networked workstations, either via a local or wide area network, and are each represented in the VE by an avatar (i.e. a user-defined geometric form). Changes that any one user makes to the virtual product are immediately visible to all others users (including the definition of cameras, landmarks, and annotations). Users can also interact allowing them to demonstrate recent changes by pointing to, and manipulating, assemblies.

Each instance of the Virtual Product Manager has an associated user context, which by default represents the first user. This means that navigation controls will act on the first body, and events sent from the Virtual Product Manager's Assembly Manager will appear to originate from the first user. You can use the Virtual Product Manager's User Browser to identify the other dVISE users, and to change the Virtual Product Manager's user context. The Virtual Product Manager's navigation controls, for example, will then manipulate another user's virtual body. Note however that by changing the Virtual Product Manager's user context you affect only the desktop interface to dVISE; your input/output devices will still manipulate your own virtual body, and you will retain your own perspective in the dVISE View.

dVISE also allows you to define *Roles* that define behavior and immersive tools that are tailored to specific user activities. You might want to define a *Trainer* and an *Engineer* role, for example, that modify the user's behavior and tools to mirror the functions that might be performed by these two types of job. You can select a role either when you start dVISE (via command line options) or you can select roles by using the Virtual Product Manager's User Browser.

The ToolBox

For those users that elect to use immersive VR peripherals (such as head-mounted displays and 3D mice) most dVISE modules support an immersive ToolBox option—the dV/ITools option. The ToolBox is a set of 3D tools that are accessible from within the VE. It provides an immersive interface to many design and navigation aids.

Design operations that you perform using the ToolBox are defined by explicit interaction with assemblies. For example, you can select a constraint tool and an assembly in the environment and constrain the assembly by making natural 3D movements. You assign other attributes, such as lighting and audio, using similar interactive tools. You can animate an assembly by simply selecting it and pointing to positions that define the required motion.

You can configure the ToolBox to include the tools most appropriate to your own tasks. You can also define ToolBoxes for specific activities, and associate each with a user Role. The tools required for a review of your virtual product may differ from those of a design activity, for example, so you might want to define Reviewer and Designer roles.

Using templates and libraries

A designer can make templates of assemblies and then create many instances of them in the VE. With complex assemblies this can save a lot of work as the instances inherit all of their initial properties from the templates. Inheritance also makes it easier to build complex environments; the detail is encapsulated in the assembly template and you can treat the instance as a single component or building block.

For example, you might build up a robot arm from a number of components: a base, an arm, a wrist and grippers. These components can be linked and their movements constrained to simulate the behavior of a robot. If you make this a template then you can go on to create many instances of it. Each instance inherits all the properties of the template so the links and constraints are automatically set up.

The instances can be customized by selectively changing their inherited properties, or by adding new properties. Changes that are made to the template's properties affect all instances that inherit those properties; instances that have overridden the inherited properties with new properties are unaffected.

For example, all instances of the robot arm assembly might inherit a gray color from the template, but you can selectively change some instances to another color. If you subsequently decide that you want to change the gray color, you can modify the template and implicitly change all gray instances.

Libraries

Libraries define a collection of assembly templates. A library can be defined as an integral component of a product's VDI file (in which case the templates are only applicable to one product) or it can be defined in a separate VDI file that contains only library definitions (in which case the templates are more widely available).

In addition to assembly templates the VDI file can also record key-frame templates which define animation sequences. Because animations can be complex (and time consuming to define) a designer might define a generic template that can be applied to any of the assemblies in the virtual product.

A second kind of library used by dVISE defines the materials (i.e. colors and textures) that can be applied to the surfaces' of the assemblies. Materials are defined in BMF files, and are typically derived from the CAD environment when the assemblies are converted. Material files can also be created manually, and edited, as described in the dVISE Geometry Tools User Guide.

dVISE summary

As one can see from this brief overview, dVISE has been designed to address the real problems encountered within the industrial sector. Division's knowledge of immersive and non-immersive VR systems is second to none, and dVISE is probably the most advanced VR product currently available.

Multigen

Although I have said that many VR models are imported from CAD systems, there are a number of modeling systems that are used to create 3D VEs. Perhaps one of the most well known companies in this field is Multigen, Inc., who have been producing modeling software since 1986. Their products are widely used throughout the simulation, real-time, and entertainment industries, and their OpenFlight scene description database runs on SGI, E & S, CAE, Flight Safety, Sony, Nintendo, Sega, Macintosh, PCs and many other real-time 3D platforms.

The software products include MultiGen II Pro, MultiGen Creator, MultiGen GO, and SmartScene.

MultiGen II Pro

MultiGen II Pro is a powerful interactive modeling system with many features that include:

- Extruding and surfaces of revolution
- Auto-created LOD
- Geometry control at group, object, polygon and vertex level
- Polygon sorting for fast rendering
- Modeling of interactive instruments and control devices
- Attach sounds to 3D geometry
- Populate any selected area of the database with objects
- Data reduction
- Real-time preview
- Fog, lights, and weather effects.

MultiGen Creator

MultiGen's Creator system is founded on the OpenFlight scene description database format, and has been designed to meet the specific needs of the 3D, real-time, visualization and simulation developer. Application areas include computer game development, architectural visualization, training simulators, and military simulation. Some of features include:

- Modeling low polygon objects
- Collision detection
- Interactive texture mapping
- Free-form deformation of objects
- Associate sounds to 3D geometry
- Level of detail creation and preview
- Spatial culling to fast rendering.

MultiGen SmartScene

MultiGen SmartScene users immersive VR to build a 3D database. The user wears a two-handed Fakespace Pinch Glove interface, and HMD, and interactively manipulates objects, textures, colors and lights using hand gestures. The tasks of positioning, scaling, and rotating objects are done simultaneously in a single hand gesture. Pinch Gloves use fingertip touch pads that provide the functionality of two four-button mice.

Multigen summary

As I have mentioned earlier, it is pointless for a VR system manufacturer to duplicate the 3D modeling tools currently available. Companies such as Multigen have over a decade's experience in designing and perfecting such software tools, and it is futile attempting to compete with them. Multigen's software products have had an enormous impact upon the simulation industry, and their OpenFlight standard is a ubiquitous format for representing 3D databases.

Summary

In this chapter I have attempted to show that software is the key to any successful VR system. Such software is very complex as it integrates the areas of 3D geometric databases, rendering, interaction, navigation, 3D tracking, graphics peripherals, sound, human factors, and interface design, all running in real time. But users of VR systems want much more than this. They want to use a VR system within their own area of specialism, which could be anything from a computer game to inspecting a CAD database of an offshore oil platform! This has meant that VR companies have had to develop generic software tools that can be applied to a wide variety of disciplines, which is no mean task.

I described Superscape's VRT system and Division's dVISE system as they address two complementary markets. No doubt other software products will appear in the future, but the reader should be under no illusion that current software tools can solve all of today's problems. We have only just started to make inroads into this exciting subject of VR, and much more software has to be written.

In the next chapter we will explore various VR applications, and discover how the software requirement of one application is totally different to another.

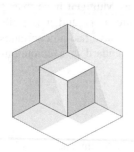

7

VR Applications

Introduction

In the 1970s when computers first started to make some sort of impact, it was possible to see that their application would have long term ramifications upon all sorts of sectors. And although it was difficult to predict exactly what would happen, one knew that the world would never be the same again. Information systems, mathematical computation, graphic design, engineering design, aerospace, architecture, control systems, telecommunications, accounting, stock markets, and even fine art were all destined to be innocent victims for computerization.

In spite of some mistakes, it was an exciting period of discovery where so-called "computer experts" learned about their craft with every system they implemented. Software tools were very primitive and system design methodologies were invented *ad hoc*.

Almost thirty years later we can look back on this period with some satisfaction, for today the computer has become the most influential technological invention in human endeavor. Computers are everywhere, and we use them in all aspects of our daily lives. Today, we do not have to argue the case for using computers—it is a forgone conclusion that a computer solution is probably the best solution.

Now that our lives revolve around computers we are in the midst of a mini revolution: virtual reality. VR, like computers, will touch everything to do with our daily lives, but it will not happen overnight. Like the early computer systems, VR will require time to mature before it can be applied effectively. Software, standards, interfaces are all issues that must be addressed if VR is to become a ubiquitous technology. But we can't just sit back and wait for these issues to be resolved—we must discover everything about VR in order to understand its strengths and weaknesses to influence its future.

Fortunately for everyone, some very dedicated people have realized that the only way to progress VR is to become involved and push the subject forward. But apart from pushing from within, VR needs to be pulled by the sectors that will eventually benefit from its use. It cannot be left to such a small industry to understand how every industrial sector can use their technology and develop appropriate software tools—it must be a joint effort.

To a certain extent this is now happening and various industries are exploring how best to use VR within their own sector. However, we must interpret carefully how such projects are progressing: great strides are being made, but VR is still an emerging technology, and we must learn to accept that it cannot be rushed.

With these thoughts in mind let us explore potential application areas for VR. The list will not be exhaustive but it will provide the opportunity to discuss a whole range of issues associated with VR and the way it's applied. Some of the examples are based upon real case studies, whilst others are anticipating future scenarios.

Industrial

Today, CAD is an important tool for industry, and the idea of using a virtual representation of a 3D object is nothing new. Computers are used on a daily basis to design everything from a single gear to an entire aircraft. Some CAD workstations can manipulate 3D objects in real time, but as these databases become very large, real-time manipulation is very difficult.

An engineer does not have to be persuaded of the importance of 3D visualization. Anything that minimizes the introduction of errors has to be considered, for the last thing anyone wants to commission is the production of an expensive tool, molding or pressing, only to discover a design fault.

One of the major advantages of CAD is the ability to visualize an object before it is manufactured, but VR enables us to get one step closer by inspecting it in real time with the aid of a suitable display. However this facility cannot be arbitrarily interfaced to the CAD process—it must be an integral feature. This will take time, but it is highly likely that VR visualization and inspection will become a standard feature of future CAD systems.

Typical industrial applications for VR include:

- visualizing engineering concepts
- training personnel
- evaluating ergonomic issues
- visualizing virtual prototypes
- exploring servicing strategies
- simulating the interaction of assemblies
- simulating the dynamics of articulated structures
- stress analysis
- distributed product development management
- simulating manufacturing processes
- collaborative engineering on large AEC projects
- machining and pressing simulation
- concurrent engineering.

It is impossible to explore all of the above to the depth they deserve, but let us examine the idea of servicing, ergonomic, virtual prototypes and visualizing engineering concepts

Servicing using a virtual prototype

Prior to CAD, engineering design involved designing and building a prototype before commissioning the tools to manufacture the real thing. The physical prototype was quite useful as it gave people something to relate to when considering its size, weight, center of gravity, mechanical handling, manufacturing and servicing issues. In many cases CAD made the physical prototype redundant, and substituted a virtual prototype in its place. With ever-increasing confidence in CAD, engineers are now able to bypass this design stage and save time and money. However, some structures being designed using CAD are very complex, and require careful examination before proceeding to the production stage. In some instances, such as the aero engine industry, a physical prototype is constructed to verify the CAD model. With engines costing millions of dollars each, manufacturing, servicing and operational issues have to be taken very seriously.

It is ironic though, that having used a computer to construct a complete virtual engine, a physical model has to be built to confirm the design! Alas this is so, but hopefully VR will provide a solution to avoid this expensive process. For instance, if the engine's database could be input into a VR system it would be possible to interact with various components and explore issues of manufacture and servicing. Although the principle is sound, it is not quite as easy as this. To begin with the database is extremely large and is not in a format readily accepted by a VR system. But filters are available to make this conversion. The size of the database is a serious problem and currently the only way to process it is in partitions. Nevertheless, sufficient research has been undertaken to show that it is possible to perform specific tasks at a virtual level that confirm it is possible to assemble and service the engine.

One approach is to view the virtual engine using a HMD and interactive glove. Then with the aid of collision detection, attempt to retrieve various pipes and components without colliding with any other components. But anyone who has serviced a car will know only too well, that the major problem of undoing the simplest nut is access for one's arm and hand, and getting sufficient torque to the spanner. If VR is to be of any use to the aero engine industry it must be able to simulate such maneuvers accurately.

Division Ltd. provided an original solution to this problem by introducing a virtual mannequin into their dVISE software. The immersed user stands alongside their 'Manikin Fred' and trains it to undertake a certain task. Whilst Fred manipulates a component with its arm and hand, the system looks for any interference with the database. When Fred is able to retrieve the component without collisions, it can be instructed to repeat the maneuver whilst the operator observes it from different points of view. Fig. 7.1 shows a view of the Rolls Royce Trent 800 engine, which has been used to evaluate the use of VR techniques in its servicing requirements, and Plate 11 shows two mannequins interacting with the VR database.

The idea of the mannequin is a very powerful interactive paradigm and is explored further in the next example.

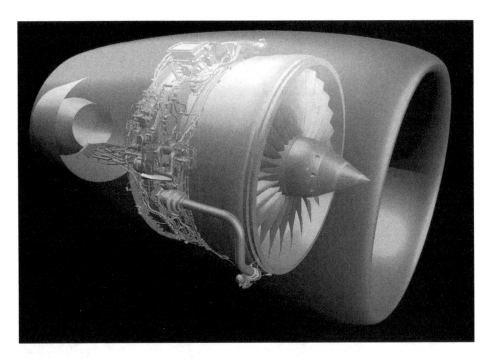

Fig. 7.1 *Rolls Royce Trent 800 engine.*
(Image courtesy of Virtual Presence)

Ergonomics

If we are to abandon physical mockups, whether they are areo engines or bulldozers, then some ergonomic issues will have to be conducted at a virtual level. This does not mean that we will be able to sit on a virtual chair and discover if it is comfortable or not; or sit inside a virtual car and feel the virtual leather steering wheel! However, it does mean that we can place a virtual person on a virtual chair and discover whether their feet touch the ground; whether their back is strained; and whether there is support for their head. It also means that we can place our virtual driver inside a virtual car and discover if they can reach the steering wheel, and whether they have a safe view of the road. These seem impossible tasks but they are all possible, and much more!

For example, Fig. 7.2 shows Division's dVise software being used to evaluate an F1 car. The Manikin Fred, can be seated in the car and used to explore optimum positions for foot pedals, steering wheel and instrumentation. It is also a simple exercise to see what Fred sees from his position.

Transom Jack

Transom Jack (TJ) is another solution to ergonomic problems and comes in the form of a biomechanically accurate human figure that works inside a VE. TJ was born in the Center for Human Modeling and Simulation at the University of Pennsylvania, and is now marketed by Transom Corporation.

Fig. 7.2 *Manikin Fred being used to evaluate an F1 car.*
(Image courtesy of Division)

TJ is used to resolve issues of fit and comfort, visibility, ingress and egress, reaching and grasping, foot pedal operation, multi-person interaction, user maintenance and strength assessment. And when TJ is undertaking any of these tasks it is possible to look through his eyes and see exactly what is seen. When TJ walks, he moves with accurate body behavior and balance control. And when TJ grasps an object, he uses fully articulated hands and 15 automatic grasps that adapt finger position to the object.

TJ has the following characteristics:

- TJ has 74 segments, 73 joints, a realistic 22-segment spine, and 150 DOF.
- TJ is derived from anthropometric data validated by the ANSUR 88 survey.
- TJ's dimensions are based on 132 anthropometric measurements.
- TJ can be customized based on scaling.
- TJ obeys joint and strength limits taken from NASA studies.
- TJ can be represented as a stick figure, wireframe, shaded, transparent or solid.

Fig. 7.3 shows TJ evaluating ergonomic issues when servicing an aircraft, and Fig. 7.4 shows TJ being used to evaluate access to components.

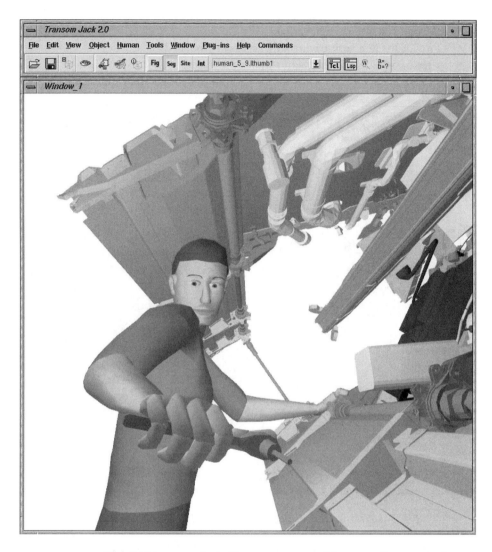

Fig. 7.3 Transom Jack. *(Image courtesy of Transom Corporation)*

Virtual prototypes

No one would dispute the importance of the virtual domain created by CAD systems. But this domain is now been extended by VR in all sorts of directions—in particular, the way it adds value at all stages in the product life cycle. Division refers to this as the 'Universal Virtual Product' which brings the following advantages:

- Provide rapid prototyping of early concepts.
- Provide a presentation medium for managers and customers.
- Reduce the need for detailed physical prototypes.
- Improve product ergonomics and functionality.

- Support concurrent engineering.
- Provide manufacturing with early access to product details.
- Create cost-effective interactive training manuals.
- Provide a cost-effective way to present product configuration and aesthetics.

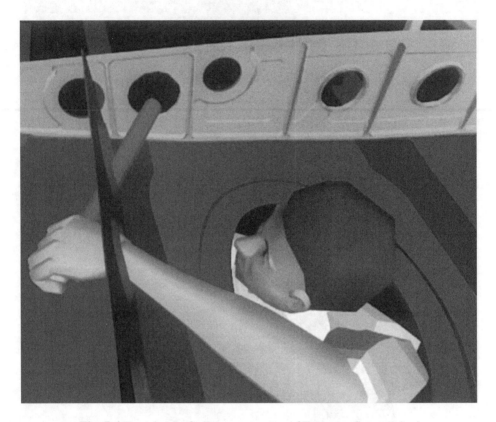

Fig. 7.4 *Transom Jack. (Image courtesy of Transom Corporation)*

The universality introduced by this design methodology supports collaborative design, and provides everyone with an increased understanding of complex 3D assemblies.

Designers today no longer work in the same building: they may be on another site 30 miles away, or even in another country 3,000 miles away. They may even work for another company sub-contracted to perform designated tasks. Managing such a distributed network requires a new ideas, new tools, and new working modalities. But central to everything is computer software.

Division recognized early on that VR was the key to this problem and configured their dVISE software product to support this process. Some of dVISES's major features are summarized in Table 7.1.

To support the concept of a Universal Virtual Product (UVP) dVISE includes four modules: dV/Reality, dV/Review, dV/Player and dV/Manikin.

Table 7.1 *Characteristics of Division's dVISE system.*

Universal Virtual Product using dVISE	
Real-time performance	Real-time fly-through of large databases.
3D interaction	Ability to pick and move objects.
Collision detection	Real-time detection of colliding parts.
CAD link	Runtime link to Pro/Engineer or Unigraphics.
Moving parts	Create very complex assemblies/disassembles.
Animation	Create and study assembly/disassembly sequences.
Behavior	Create complex physical simulations.
Collaboration	Support multi-user (collaborative) sessions.
Assemblies	View and edit entire assembly trees.
Joints and linkages	Create joints between parts.
Image fidelity	Create realistic images with materials & textures.
Audio	Define realistic audio properties.
Part information	Create part data lists.
Selective importing	Only load those parts of an assembly you need.
3D support	Supports 3D projection, CrystalEyes & Spaceball.
Immersion	Support optional full immersion.

dV/Reality

Supports the creation of the UVP by providing Zone Managers that address:

- Creating and managing Zone structure within a database.
- Importing and managing different sub-assemblies, e.g. importing supplier assemblies from different CAD systems into a design cell.

Advanced Design Engineers for defining:

- Assembly/disassembly animations and sequences.
- Simple component linkages.
- Behaviors.

And developing interactive training tools.

The dVISE Behavior Engine

Throughout this book I have emphasized the role simulation can play in VR—and here is an area where its benefits cannot be ignored. In this industrial setting the idea of *smart parts* has been created by dVISE's behavior engine. A smart part is a virtual object with 'intelligence'. For example, say that you need to position a reservoir for the windshield wipers. There is a trade off between height above the ground, and size of pump power. You can create a smart reservoir, that will take as inputs the pump power, height below the outlet nozzle, and length of pipe required reaching the nozzle via the pump. Every time the user moves the reservoir, an event is generated that causes the reservoir to re-calculate the pressure of the water exciting the outlet. This pressure can then be displayed as a 3D dial attached to the reservoir, or any part of the assembly. So now as the designer moves the reservoir around, he or she can see in real time the effect on water pressure at the outlet. Using similar 'smart' techniques it is even possible to create parts that will analyze their surroundings and automatically move to an optimal position.

Smart parts can be used for optimizing many different aspects of a design: checking locality of electrical components, weight distribution, accessibility, color optimization, etc.

The behavior engine also allows you to simulate product functionality. Create controls: buttons, levers, etc. that accurately control the intended components, e.g. create a virtual tractor cab, where all the levers accurately control the position of front loader, bucket, grab, etc. Simulate the effects of various valves in the cooling system of your power plant, and allow the operator or trainee to study the effect of varying these valves.

Plate 10 illustrates a virtual earth-moving vehicle manufactured by John Deere. Division's dVISE software was used to assess its functionality using a VR system. The dV/Reality tools were used to connect the vehicle's controls so that it could be operated from within the cabin. Looking through the operator's eyes it is possible to see exactly what a real operator would see in practice.

dV/Review

dV/Review allows the designer to view the full product structure, as well as fly-through, walk-through, and interact with the UVP. It also provides an intuitive interface to pick up and move components in 3D to facilitate the study of form and fit, and it is possible to browse the assembly structure (tree) to review product structure. You can also play and control complex assembly/disassembly sequences, and run a complete simulation of the product functionality, e.g. see how the engine ignition sequence works, and interact with it.

dV/Review also offers a collaborative design capability, which enables multiple users to concurrently view and interact with the same assembly. An avatar (user definable) represents each user in the collaborative session, and individuals can pick up parts, move them around, and hand them one to another.

It is possible to selectively load and unload components/assemblies in the assembly structure tree to control what is being visualized. This enables selective visualization of very large assemblies even on PC based platforms.

When problems are found in the design, an annotation tool enables notes to be left, to notify other users of the potential problems.

Any number of view positions or landmarks can be established, so that you can jump to a pre-defined location, such as the engine bay at the press of a button.

dV/Player

dV/Player is the basic kernel of the dVISE product range, and is a general-purpose player for a wide range of 3D applications: including product fly-through and review, buildings walk-throughs, interactive training environments, product point of sale systems, etc.

It is designed to allow real-time navigation of very large environments, and employs real-time database management techniques to control the complexity of what is viewed. dV/Player allows a single component or a large assembly, or the whole vehicle, to be viewed, and to quickly switch between these.

But dV/Player offers more than just fly-through of your data. You can play and control complex assembly/disassembly sequences, you can run a complete simulation of the product functionality, e.g. see how the engine ignition sequence works, and interact with it.

dV/Player provides a 3D view or window onto the UVP, and you can navigate within this window with a 2D mouse. However there is no 2D graphical user interface to view the assembly hierarchy, or to modify any component of the assembly.

dV/Player is also Netscape Navigator pluggable and so you can embed your UVPs within HTML documents, and publish them on the Web. Any Web user can then access and view the UVP from Navigator. See Fig. 7.5.

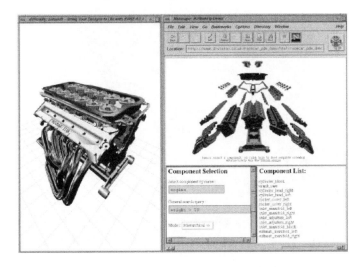

***Fig. 7.5** Using the Netscape browser to visualize a CAD database.*
(Image courtesy of Division)

dV/Manikin

dV/Manikin is an optional add on to the dV/Reality package. It provides the designer with the ability to add manikins to the UVP to study various ergonomic issues. dV/Manikin allows you to study, reachability, visibility, and collision free access. A library of male Manikins is available to study the effect of specific population sizes.

The male Manikin Fred can be rapidly manipulated in the environment using only a 2D mouse. You can move the whole body or individual limbs, and Fred obeys realistic joint constraints. You can also control Fred with goal oriented events. So Fred can be asked to walk forward, reach up, turn round, etc. Fred will also react to environmental conditions, for example upon colliding with other components Fred will stop his current action. Fred also supports a range of gestures such as: grasp, drop, pick, as well as supporting a selective grasp with which he will curl his fingers in to grasp an object until each finger collides with the object.

Virtual weapons

GDE Systems and the U.S. Army Armament Research Development and Engineering Center (ARDEC) are using VR to optimize the design of virtual weapons. Such weapons are based on 3D solid models imported from Pro-Engineer CAD/CAM software. The models are integrated into a VE using Division's dVISE VR software running on an SGI Onyx workstation, and a HMD.

Several weapons are undergoing evaluation with VR at ARDEC, including the Objective Individual Combat Weapon (OICW) and the M198 towed howitzer. The OICW is a multi-purpose, hand-held weapon and the VR simulation allows a user to interact with an urban scenario using a stereolithography model of the OICW.

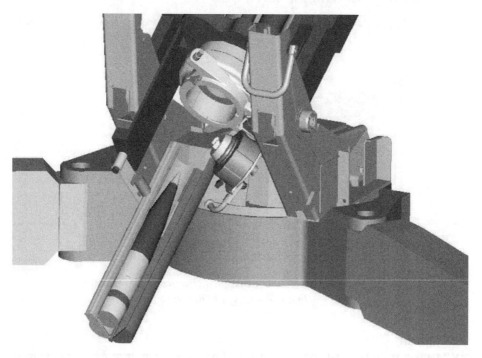

Fig. 7.6 The M198 howitzer. (Image courtesy of Division)

The M198 howitzer (Fig. 7.6) simulation allows users to examine concept autoloader operations under battlefield-type conditions. As a result, ARDEC is capable of evaluating the feasibility of various autoloader designs. The OICW and M198 VR simulations, along with others under development, will ultimately become an integral part of ARDEC's Distributed Interactive Simulation (DIS) node. This will allow users to be immersed in a simulated battlefield using hardware that is still in the concept development stage.

Visual engineering

The Cadcentre at Cambridge, UK, has pioneered the use of CAD since its inception. Today, they have embraced the technology of VR and are pioneering the use of group VR in process plant design using their Review Reality software, and the use of a panoramic screen.

The Cadcentre's PDMS (Plant Design Management System) is used throughout the world in the design of offshore platforms, chemical processing plant, oil refineries, nuclear facilities, etc. But a PDMS database can now be used by Review Reality to visualize massive 3D structures in real time. The advantages are enormous, as it makes it easier for project staff and other personnel to assess and become familiar with design proposals, planned operational changes, maintenance tasks, and escape routes.

Plate 17 shows a view of the Caister Murdoch gas compression platform generated using the Cadcentre's Review Reality System. This can be viewed in real time, using realistic texture maps, shadows, and anti-aliasing, and at the same time it is possible to make cross-sectional views and make interactive measurements.

Spatial Visualization

Visualizing spatial problems is what VR is about. Whether it is trying to understand the 3D electrical bonds of a complex molecule or navigating the interior of a proposed offshore oil platform. VR provides intuitive ways for exploring 3D environments, no matter what they may be.

One such visualization problem that faces any industry is factory reorganization. It is a complex process as it involves optimizing parameters such as overall efficiency, machine accessibility, health and safety, services, etc. But it is the 3D nature of the problem that makes finding an optimum solution so difficult. Now VR is no magic wand, but it does provide a means for solving such problems effectively.

Such techniques are used regularly by PERA to solve 3D spatial problems. They have at their disposal a variety of VR tools that include PCs, workstations, supercomputers, immersive HMD systems, and wide screen systems. A recent project involved redeveloping the internal production facility for Northern Foods. They wanted a further automated line in place of an existing manually intensive one, and the opportunity to reorganize the production flow.

PERA provided a detailed visualization of the entire production process, a means of delivering off-line training and familiarization, and a visual production process simulation. The simulation was able to review the space utilization and production layout to assist the installation of the new production equipment and rearrangement of the existing plant. Site facilities such as drains, water supplies and structural limitations were simulated and taken into account when positioning the new lines. All of this was done at a virtual level, in real time, avoiding any disruptions in factory production. Fig. 7.7 shows an image from the real-time simulation of the factory production facility.

A similar problem was resolved by PERA when they were commissioned to simulate the new headquarters for Barclaycard. Barclaycard wanted their staff to see what their working environment would be like before they started construction. PERA took the

CAD database of the architectural model and input it into their VR system. Some of the 2500 Barclaycard staff had the opportunity to view the virtual building and input ideas on the design of the offices, including floor layout, color schemes, furnishing and accessibility. Fig. 7.8 shows a scene from the simulation.

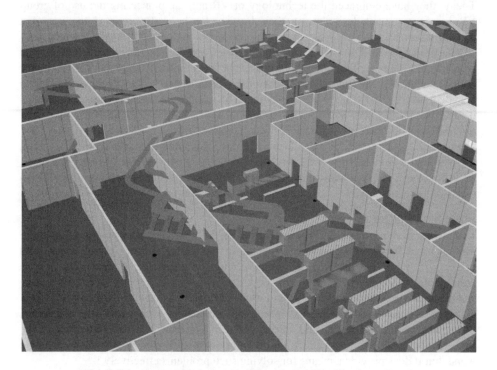

***Fig. 7.7** A simulated production plant layout for Northern Foods.*
(Image courtesy of PERA)

Training simulators

Simulators play a vital role in training personnel in all sorts of sectors, and include airplanes, trains, lorries, tanks, medicine, ships, air traffic control towers, nuclear power stations, military weapons, etc. They are very effective and are used in areas where the only alternative is the actual system, which would be far too dangerous.

The two applications selected for further description are medicine and aviation.

Medicine

Computers have had an incredible impact upon medicine and health care, ranging from automatic systems to monitor patients to the image processing of 3D CT data. But one application that has captured everyone's imagination is surgical training, and the role VR could play in simulating virtual organs, or an entire virtual cadaver.

Fig. 7.8 *A scene from a real-time simulation for Barclaycard's new HQ.*
(Image courtesy of PERA)

Soft body modeling

There are some very difficult problems to overcome before we see VR systems widely used throughout the medical profession. The first one concerns the modeling of flesh and simulating its behavior. The 3D models we have discussed in previous chapters were rigid, and in some cases incorporated articulated features. It is possible to model non-rigid bodies using triangles, but instead of using triangles of a fixed size, their size is allowed to change depending upon the forces applied the their vertices.

For example, in Fig. 7.9 a mesh of 3D triangles are interconnected with an element that changes its distance depending upon applied forces. Internally, the element has elastic and resistive properties that can be adjusted to simulate a variety of elastic materials. This is a useful strategy for modeling cloth and boundary surfaces that have elastic properties. However, because the mesh forms a thin skin, its interior is empty and is not convenient to model a solid piece of flesh. Another approach is to model a 3D lattice of points that are interconnected with the same elements, as shown in Fig. 7.10.

When forces are applied to the lattice nodes, the 3D geometry adjusts to an appropriate new shape. And when the forces are removed, the geometry returns to its original shape, and could even oscillate slightly to simulate real world behavior. What is important is to adjust the element's parameters to achieve a desired behavior.

If the lattice structure is very fine it is even possible to arrange for a fault to propagate across the lattice to simulate a cutting action. Thus a single lattice could be divided in two.

So basically, a strategy exists to model 3D flesh, and research is underway to perfect its implementation. In the meantime though, VR is still able to play a role in surgical training, and we will take a brief look at a VR based laparoscopic simulator.

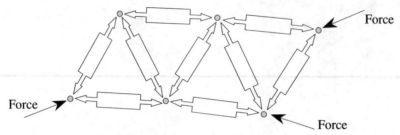

Fig. 7.9 *A flexible 3D triangular mesh.*

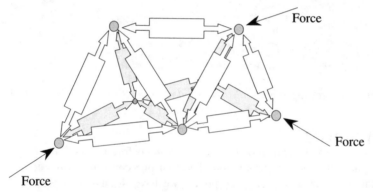

Fig. 7.10 *A flexible 3D lattice.*

Minimally Invasive Surgery

Minimally Invasive Surgery, or keyhole surgery using its popular name, is a surgical procedure that minimizes patient trauma by keeping body incisions as small as possible. In many cases, the incision is no more than 1 or 2 cm in diameter—just enough room to insert a surgical instrument. Because the incision is so small the surgeon is unable to see what is taking place within the body's cavity, therefore another incision is made through which is passed an endoscope. The video output of the endoscope is displayed upon a monitor and provides the surgeon with an internal view of the patient and the end of the keyhole instrument.

Naturally, this requires the surgeon to undertake surgical maneuvers by looking at a screen rather than their hands, and calls for a different level of eye-hand spatial coordination. Furthermore, the endoscope provides a magnified view of the patient's interior and a narrow field of view.

In order to acquire the extra skills for keyhole surgery, surgeons use various physical training devices. These consist of simple trainers where a surgeon has to perform various tasks such as suturing, peeling grapes, manipulating small objects, etc. using laparoscopic tools. More sophisticated simulators use animal meat, and in some countries, live animals are used.

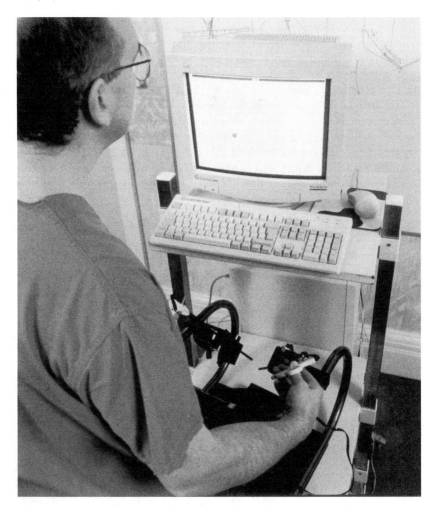

Fig. 7.11 *The MIST trainer in action. (Image courtesy of Virtual Presence)*

In the early 1990s various VR based laparoscopic simulators emerged but failed to convince the medical sector that a solution had been found. Today, things have improved and there is a deeper understanding of what the medical profession requires. It is still impossible to simulate gall bladders, hearts, kidneys and other organs with the fidelity of their physical counterparts, and that will not happen for some years to come. However, we have reached a point where simple VR simulators can play a valuable role in the overall training task.

One such device is MIST (Minimally Invasive Surgical Training) from Virtual Presence Ltd. The system (Fig. 7.11) comprises of a frame holding two standard laparscopic instruments, which are electronically linked, to a high-performance computer. MIST software constructs a VE on the screen showing the position and movement of the surgical instruments in real time.

In training mode, the program guides the trainee through a series of six tasks that become progressively more complex, enabling him/her to develop psychomotor skills essential for safe clinical practice. Each task is based on a key surgical technique employed in minimally invasive surgery. An on-line help facility, which includes video clips of live procedures, enables the trainee to relate the virtual task to its clinical context. The help facility also enables the trainee to use the system independently of the tutor. Performance is scored for time, errors and efficiency of movement for each task, and for both right and left hands. This information is available on completion of the tasks for the trainee, and is stored to the database for review by the tutor.

The ultimate goal for laparscopic simulators is to provide realistic force feedback from the surgical instruments, realistic 3D VEs, running in real time on a low cost platform.

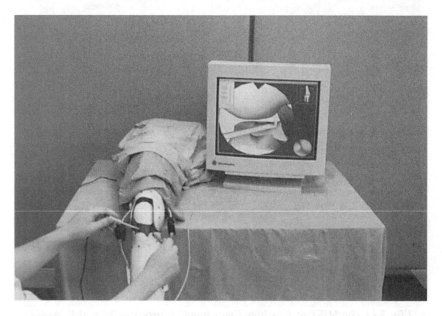

Fig. 7.12 An arthroscopic simulator.(Image courtesy of University of Hull)

A similar type of simulator has been developed at the University of Hull, but simulates surgical operations upon the knee. Fig. 7.12 shows the simulator in action. It consists of an artificial knee with appropriate keyhole instruments. On the table, the trainee surgeon observes the interior of a virtual knee, complete with virtual instruments. As the real instruments are manipulated, tracking devices hidden within the false knee relay their position to a host computer that responds in real time with an updated view of the virtual knee.

It is not difficult to appreciate the importance of these systems, and as computers become cheaper and new software systems developed, VR simulators will become a natural part of any surgeon's training.

Readers who are interested in finding out more about this exciting subject should look at the following references: www.cine-med.com, www.vrweb.com, www.ht.com, www.shef.ac.uk/~vrmbg/arthro1.html (Holton and Alexander, 1995).

Virtual therapy

For those suffering from acrophobia (fear of heights) the Kaiser-Permanente Medical Group in Marin County, California offers an interesting treatment using VR. Dr. Ralph Lamson at the medical group used 90 volunteers in an experimental study, of whom, 90% reached their self-assigned "height goals".

The volunteers were placed in a VE where they encountered the perception of depth and height. The environment depicted a café with an elevated patio and plank leading from the patio to a bridge. Surrounding hills and water completed the scene. Forty-four of the participants in the study were selected randomly to immerse themselves in this environment using Division's Pro Vision 100 VR system.

Under the guidance of Lamson, each volunteer was given a HMD that depicted the VE. The challenge was to exit the café onto the patio, move across the plank, and explore the bridge. As they approached the edge of the plank and the bridge and looked at the landscape below, heart rate and blood pressure were measured to monitor the level of anxiety.

After successfully "surviving" their virtual encounter with heights and depths, the participants graduated to real-world goals, such as driving across a bridge and going inside a glass enclosed elevator while looking outside.

Civilian flight simulators

Throughout this book I have referred to the way the flight simulation industry paved the way for many VR techniques, so maybe it's time to elaborate slightly on this application.

A flight simulator has two important roles: one is to assess the technical competence of qualified pilots, and the other is to familiarize qualified pilots with a new craft. Flight simulators are expensive (typically $10m), and their running costs are equally high; consequently their usage has to be carefully organized.

Inside the simulator is a replica cockpit of a specific aircraft. The layout and dimensions of every instrument and panel are so accurate, that it is easy to accept it as the real thing—even though it may only be constructed from wood! The instruments are connected to a computer that simulates the complete behavior of the plane: from the heat characteristics of the engines to the pneumatic properties of the undercarriage. Thus when a pilot starts the virtual engines, the relevant instruments respond with their temperature and fuel consumption.

This computer is able to replicate the electrical and mechanical properties of the plane, but another computer is required to create the images seen through the cockpit window. Although it is a computer, it is dedicated to the task of image generation—hence its name, *Image Generator* (IG). A VE of an airport and the surrounding terrain are loaded into the IG, together with the position of the simulated plane. Then, as the pilot goes through a takeoff procedure, the IG is updated with the changing position of the plane and responds with appropriate images at 60 Hz. As the plane gathers speed down the runway, another computer is waiting to simulate the flying characteristics of the craft using a mathematical model provided by the plane's manufacturer. As soon as the pilot maneuvers the plane into a takeoff attitude, the virtual plane leaves the virtual runway and the mathematical flying model takes over.

Meanwhile, during the takeoff, the IG has been supplied with the real-time position of the virtual plane, and has responded with realistic images that surround the cockpit 150° horizontally and 50° vertically. The pilot is inside a cockpit that is indistinguishable from the real thing; there are real-time collimated images outside the cockpit windows; the cabin resonates to the surround sound of jet engines; and a 6-DOF motion platform moves the ten-ton platform to provide accurate motion cues. This is real immersion! Fig. 2.12 shows a modern full flight simulator.

But in such a mission, a pilot and co-pilot are being assessed to see if they can cope with the unexpected. And inside the cabin is a trainer—an experienced pilot, whose role is to perform the assessment process. His task is relatively easy, because inside the cabin, out of sight from the pilots, is a touch sensitive screen that connects to the IG and the host computers. Simply by touching part of the screen, the trainer can activate a virtual engine fire, a faulty undercarriage, a leaking fuel pump, etc., and then waits to observe how the pilot and co-pilot respond. The touch screen can also be used to interact with the 3D VE: another plane can be moved onto the runway during a landing scenario; another plane can be flown along a collision course; and even a storm can be introduced and cover the runway with virtual snow! Fig. 7.13 shows the cockpit interior of a Boeing 767-300 full flight simulator used by the Royal Brunei Airlines.

The VEs will comprise an airport and the surrounding terrain, and can easily cover 50 square miles, which requires several levels of detail. For example, when the plane is making a final approach to the runway, the terrain below can consist of an aerial or satellite photograph of the area. In the distance, the pilot sees the airport and its illuminated runway, which are modeled at low resolution to keep the polygon count to a minimum. As the airport becomes larger, extra detail is faded in to reveal new features of buildings. Finally, when the plane touches the runway, the motion platform responds with an appropriate movement, and forces are fed back through the flight controls. As the pilot drives towards a terminal building, the IG is checking to ensure that the virtual wings are not touching buildings or any other planes. When the plane finally comes to a halt in front of the docking station, one can even see virtual people inside the terminal pushing their luggage along corridors, just to complete the picture. Fig. 7.14 shows a scene depicting a virtual airport as the simulated plane approaches its docking area.

The entire experience is overwhelming—and it has to be—for without this attention to detail, it would not be possible to create the necessary level of presence and immersion that make the flight simulator such an effective training tool.

Fig. 7.13 *Royal Brunei Airlines Boeing 767-300 Full Flight Simulator.*
(Image courtesy Thomson Training & Simulation)

Fig. 7.14 *Airport scene produced by an E&S IG. (Image courtesy of Evans &*
Sutherland Computer Corporation, Salt Lake City, Utah, USA)

*Fig. 7.15 A 3D database derived from a satellite image. (Image courtesy of Evans &
Sutherland Computer Corporation, Salt Lake City, Utah, USA)*

Military flight simulators

Military flight simulators rely upon similar technology, but tend to use a dome as the
display surface, as this replicates the all-round vision they have in a modern fighter.
More projectors and IGs are required to cover the extra surface of the dome, but they do
not have to display high-resolution images. By tracking the pilot's eyes, it is possible to
have a medium-resolution background image with a high-resolution gaze image. Thus
wherever the pilot looks, there will be appropriate detail.

In combat, pilots are flying extremely fast and must be familiar with the surrounding
terrain, which means that the mission rehearsal simulator must also reflect this level of
accuracy. To resolve this problem, satellite images are used, that provide height as well
as texture information. When processed by software tools such as E&S's
RapidScene/Freedom, it is possible to convert a numerical data file into a realistic
terrain as seen in Fig. 7.15.

Entertainment

Real-time computer graphics plays a central role in computer games, arcade games and theme park experiences. In all three markets the technology is carefully chosen to entertain and create profit. Computer games cost about $50 and can provide many hours of entertainment—even the game station is relatively cheap. Arcade games cost many times more but have to be much more robust and offer a more thrilling experience, and succeed in enticing the punter to have 'just one more go' in an attempt to improve upon a previous record.

Some early attempts to introduce immersive VR entertainment systems into the marketplace failed because of irreconcilable commercial factors. For example, a computer graphics workstation was often used as the real-time source of images, which immediately made it impossible to recoup its cost, let alone any other important features. When cheaper graphics boards emerged and low-cost HMDs were designed, it still seemed impossible to maintain the necessary throughput to generate a valid commercial return. But as the VR industry progresses, new and hopefully commercially viable products are appearing.

Dream Glider and Sky Explorer

Dreamality Technologies, Inc. is a manufacturer of VR based simulators for hang gliding, paragliding, ultralights and other aviation simulators. Their Dream Glider system replicates the performance of an actual hang glider, and is used by new hang glider pilots to improve their flying skills.

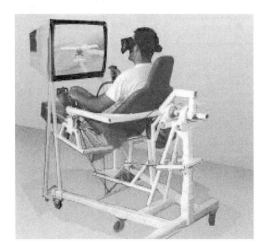

Fig. 7.16 *The Sky Explorer motion based simulator.*
(Courtesy Dreamality Technologies)

The rider is free to fly anywhere within a VE, and a scoring system encourages the rider to fly to a landing area and land safely. The rider scores points for finding thermals and gaining altitude, the length of flying time, and for successful landings. The scoring system also deducts points for crashes and collisions with weather phenomena and objects such as planes, jets, birds, balloons, ultralights, buildings, etc.

The Dream Glider is PC based and allows the rider to experience the normal flying sensations of sound, tactile, motion cues and visual feedback. When using a HMD, head tracking can be used to permit the rider to look in any direction, and when networked to other simulators, each rider can see fellow riders in their environment.

The ultralight Sky Explorer is a motion-based simulator with pitch and roll in the basic product. Fig. 7.16 shows the motion system which includes throttle and rudder pedals.

The Sky Explorer can also be networked with the Dream Glider so that users can see each other in their own visual display. They can interact with each other, fly coordinated maneuvers, or even try to knock each other out of their virtual skies! The VEs currently available include: Space, Islands, Jungle, Volcano, Castles, Obstacles, Swamp, Frontier, Prehistoric and City, which is depicted in Fig. 7.17.

Fig. 7.17 Dream Glider and Sky Explorer exploring a city VE.
(Image courtesy of Dreamality Technologies)

Venturer S2i

Entertainment simulators have been a great commercial success, especially in theme parks where sixty people at a time, share a 4-minute passive experience that consists of an exciting film ride supported with sound and motion. Although this would not be classed as VR, the technique does use immersion, motion and computer-generated images to create a synthetic experience. Smaller simulators also exist where a dozen-or-so people can enjoy the same experience.

Until recently, the technology cost implications prevented smaller simulators from being manufactured, but with the availability of low-cost PCs and cheap motion platforms, two-seater simulators are appearing. One of the most recent interactive simulators is the S2i from Thomson Entertainment, shown in Plate 16. It is available with either a hydraulic or an electric motion base with 3-DOF, and players 'fly' the system using joystick or steering wheel controls. The system operates from a Windows computer platform with real-time computer graphics, and can be networked with other simulators.

Human movement analysis

The University of Teesside's VR Center is working in a variety of areas such as virtual process simulation, SME marketing, offshore/onshore environments and virtual production and planning. But one unusual project is in the area of human movement analysis, where the objective is to develop an effective motion capture model to analyze and assess human movement.

The initial motion capture system will employ a basic 3D virtual gymnast as shown in Fig. 7.18 which will be used to analyze the movement and overall performance of gymnasts. It is expected that gymnasts, judges and coaches will all benefit from the system.

In addition to its use for improving performance, the model could be used to identify and monitor the risk of injury and its prevention. On completion, the model will be made available as an online service to various sporting centers of excellence, gymnasiums, and eventually leisure facilities.

WWW Applications

It is inevitable that as industry and commerce increasingly use the WWW, new applications will be found for 3D VEs. Already a number exist and I will summarize just a few to illustrate the potential of this medium.

Virtual exhibitions
In 1997, Virtex and Electronic Telegraph, created the world's first full scale 3D exhibition on the web—Virtex 97. Today, they have opened the VEC (Virtual Exhibition Center) which hosts the updated Virtex97 IT show with over 50 exhibitors from the IT industry. Accompanying the show is a 3D Conference Center where visitors can listen to real-time streamed presentations from some of the leading companies at the show. Visit http://www.virtex.co.uk/v96demo/vtest/entfram.htm to browse the virtual exhibition.

Fig. 7.18 A virtual gymnast. (Image courtesy of University of Teesside's VR Center)

Virtual art gallery

The State of the Art virtual art gallery is a joint project by Intel, Superscape and Interated Systems. It includes works from Isa Genzken as well as pieces from the up-and-coming artists Anton Henning and Claus Goedicke. Visitors can wander through the gallery's virtual wings and view digital works in high resolution. Each piece includes a biographical sketch of the artists and comments from experts. Fractal decompression techniques have been used to minimize download times. Take a look at http://www.intel.com/english/art/.

Heritage

Intel and English Heritage have developed a fully interactive VE of Stonehenge for distribution over the Web. Developed with the guidance of English Heritage archeologists, the 3D Web Page was launched on 20 June 1996 to coincide with the summer solstice.

The screen is split to provide text on the left-hand side and the virtual 3D world on the right. Using Superscape's Viscape, you can click on words in the text and 'hot-link' to special features in the VE as well as other related areas of text. The 'Timeline' feature along the top of the screen lets you select a period in the evolution of Stonehenge that you would like to learn about. To find out more about this project, take a look at http://www.superscape.com/intel/shenge.htm.

Virtual shopping

CompuServe's VRcade, one of the new generation of Web-based on-line shopping services, is the world's first VR shopping center. Based on London's Picadilly Circus, the shopping center comprises three different virtual shopping worlds: in-town, out-of-town and underground. Visitors to the site can explore the different shops and make their purchases on-line using a credit card. Further information about virtual shopping can be found on http://www.compuserve.co.uk/shoppingcentre.

Summary

There has only been space to investigate some of the applications for VR that are currently underway. Unfortunately, some had to be left out such as architecture, fashion, automotive design, education, training, science, space, etc., and if these were your areas of specialism I apologize. But hopefully, the applications I have covered will give you an insight and the potential of VR technology in other areas.

What I have tried to do in this chapter is to show that VR has matured very quickly and offers powerful solutions to some very difficult problems. VR is no longer a technology looking for an application, it is a solution to any problem that involves the real-time visualization of complex 3D data.

It is not difficult to imagine how car-body designers, architects or fashion designers could use VR. The technology exists—it is just a question of developing appropriate software tools.

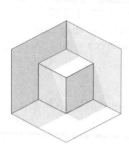

8
Conclusion

The past

It is strange to look back and recall the manual techniques used to design everything from a bracket to a complete aircraft. A large wooden drawing board with T-square, pair of compasses, a set-square, a set of plastic French curves, an eraser, etc., were the typical tools of the draftsman. Specialist skills were required in projections, cross sections, developed surfaces, and perspective views. And to obtain a realistic view of the final artifact, a technical artist was used to render a colored image.

Then computers came along, and the discipline of computer graphics was born. A new set of design tools emerged that relieved the draftsman from the tedious pencil based tasks. Computer graphics showed that it was capable of undertaking all of the manual tasks associated with 3D design, from which emerged the sophisticated CAD systems we use today.

But computer graphics did not stop evolving. Computer graphics was used to animate 2D shapes and 3D objects, and computer animation was born which blossomed into the industry of digital special effects. Another target was video and television, and the computer demonstrated amazing dexterity in its ability to manipulate real-time video. Video images could be painted, retouched, enhanced, cut and pasted, turned like a real page, until it was impossible to tell whether they were real or synthetic.

Having mastered images, computers were used to process sound, from which evolved multimedia systems to provide a unifying digital medium for text, sound and images.

But computers did not stop evolving. Faster, cheaper, smaller systems kept appearing each year, making the computerization of new markets cost effective solutions.

All of these developments were taking place against a backdrop of rapid technological advances in electronics, miniaturization, new materials, communications, etc., making possible totally new computer based systems. One of these developments was virtual reality that offered a new way of interacting with the complex 3D structures being stored inside computers.

Today

Today, we take for granted CAD systems. We don't think twice about the fact that we are using digital packets of electricity and magnetism to encode and manipulate 3D objects. Designs of buildings, cars, robots, household objects, and even circuits for new computers, are designed with such efficiency and familiarity, that one could believe it was the only way to undertake such tasks.

However, even though these systems are so effective, we continue to refine and extend these tools with even more powerful tools, one of which is VR. But as we have seen, VR is not restricted to the world of CAD—it has applications that know no boundaries. VR can be used in computer games, education, training, simulation, visualization, surgery, and a hundred-and-one other topics.

Conclusion

If you have managed to read through the previous seven chapters, you should have formed an opinion about what VR is and how it works. I have tried to present to you what I believe to be the essential elements of VR, free from any popular journalistic hype—just the facts. Now this might not have tallied with your original perception of VR, and my description may not have supported some of the fantastic stories that surround VR—but that was not my aim. Even at this stage of the book I could fantasize about the role of VR in the next millennium, but I don't know what purpose that would serve. Anyone can make predictions about the future, but when one is concerned with the present, then one must be accurate and honest.

I have shown that VR is a natural development in the progression of computer graphics. Yes, it introduces some strange concepts such as the ability to see, touch, and hear things that have no physical substance, but these experiences are obviously synthetic. VR was not developed to provide us with an alternative to the physical world—it was developed to solve specific technical problems.

We have seen that the flight simulation industry has been major users of real-time graphics for many years. They have worked with the ideas of 3D models, dynamic level-of-detail, collision detection, force-feedback, immersive displays, interactive features, etc., long before the term *virtual reality* was coined. For them, they were dealing with simulation.

But over the past decade it has become possible to implement many of these ideas on low-cost systems and apply them to a wider range of applications. But before any real serious work could be done, various books and films appeared that extrapolated VR in all sorts of directions. We were exposed to a world where we could navigate massive 3D corporate databases and cause havoc by destroying data using virtual weapons; one could wrestle with avatars; and why not be possessed by virtual intelligence! Authors and film directors created a fantastic world of virtual reality that has become confused with the *real* world of virtual reality.

I mentioned in the opening chapter that the word 'virtual' has been totally overused. And almost everyday articles appear in national newspapers concerning a new application for VR, creating an impression of a technology that is widely used in industry, commerce, medicine, training, military and entertainment. This is far from the truth. Personally I would like this to be the case, because I am totally convinced by the benefits of VR. But one cannot force a technology upon any sector, whether it is VR or any other new invention.

As I prepare the text for this last chapter, advertisements are appearing in the press announcing a new range of 500 MHz PC processors. There is no doubt that they out perform computers sold last year, but there is no way that any industry can afford to replace their existing computers with every new model that appears. The same thing is true with VR. No matter how compelling the reasons might be for using VR, it will take time to introduce VR into all of the relevant sectors of application. It will happen, and it will be a success, but it will happen in its own time.

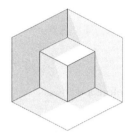

Glossary

3D Pointer The visual representation of the user's hand as distinct from the ordinary mouse or text cursor; also known as the body.

Accommodation The eye's ability to alter the shape of its lens to focus on objects near and far.

Active environment A VE that includes events that are independent of the user.

Acuity The ability to resolve fine detail.

Active matrix LCD An LCD display with pixels controlled by discrete transistors.

Additive color mixing Creating colors by mixing two or three different colored lights.

Additive primary colors Red, green and blue.

Aliasing
(a) **Spatial**: Visual artifacts such as jagged edges caused by insufficient sampling.

(b) **Temporal**: Animation artifacts, such as 'wagon wheels' apparently rotating backwards, caused by insufficient temporal sampling.

Ambient light The background level illumination introduced to illuminate a VE.

Ambisonics A technique for recording sound using a Soundfield microphone, and played back using several loudspeakers.

Anechoic Without echoes.

Angle of view The solid angle of incident light transmitted by a lens.

Angular velocity The rotational velocity about an axis.

Anti-aliasing Strategies for removing or reducing aliasing artifacts arising from insufficient spatial or temporal sampling.

Anti-clockwise polygon Has its interior to the left when its boundary is traversed in the direction of its edges.

Aspect ratio Ratio of the vertical to the horizontal dimensions of an image or shape.

Attributes   Object properties such as color, surface texture and mass.

Augmented reality   Display systems that mix synthetic images with views of the real world.

Authoring tool   See **generator**.

Avatar   The abstract representation of the user in a VE.

Back face   The unseen side of a polygon.

Back face removal   The removal of all back-facing polygons before a scene is rendered.

Back-projection screen   A translucent screen where the image is projected from behind.

Binaural   The use of two separate audio channels.

Binocular depth cues   Strategies such as eye convergence and parallax for estimating the distance of an object.

Binocular disparity   The differences between the left and right views of a scene.

Binocular vision   The ability to see two independent views of a scene.

Boom display   A display system mounted on a balanced articulated arm.

Boundary representation   A modeling strategy where objects are represented by a boundary skin.

Bounding box   A rectangular bounding volume that completely contains an object.

Bounding sphere   A spherical bounding volume that contains an object.

Browser   A computer program that interprets VRML files and allows the user to interact and navigate them.

B-spline space curve   A smooth parametric curve whose shape is determined by a string of control points.

B-spline surface patch   A smooth parametric surface patch whose shape is determined by a matrix of control points.

Bump map   A 2D image for making a surface appear bumpy.

C   A computer programming language.

C++   An object-oriented version of C.

CAD   An acronym for Computer Aided Design.

CAM   An acronym for Computer Aided Manufacture.

Cartesian coordinates   2D or 3D offset measurement relative to some defined origin and system of orthogonal axes.

Center of projection   The point through which all projection lines pass.

CFD   See **computational fluid dynamics**.

CFF   See **critical fusion frequency**.

Ciliary muscles   Adjust the shape of the human eye's lens.

Clipping   Removes unwanted objects from a scene.

Clockwise polygon   Has its interior to the right when its boundary is traversed in the direction of its edges.

Cochlea   Coverts sound pressure waves into nerve signals in the inner ear.

Collimated   A collimated optical system has light rays that appear to come from some distance.

Collision avoidance   Strategies to prevent objects from colliding.

Collision detection   Strategies to detect collisions between virtual objects.

Color attributes   Color values assigned to an object to enable it to be rendered.

Color bleeding   When the color of one object is reflected in another.

Color model   A color space such as RGB or HSV.

Computational fluid dynamics (CFD)   Simulates the dynamic flow of gas and fluid about an object.

Cone   A receptor in the retina responsible for color vision.

Constraints   Physical limits used to restrict an object's behavior.

Constructive solid geometry (CSG)   A modeling strategy for building objects using the Boolean operators: union, subtraction and difference.

Cornea   The transparent surface at the front of the eye.

CPU   An acronym for Central Processing Unit.

Critical fusion frequency   The frequency at which a flashing image appears continuous to the eye.

CRT   An acronym for Cathode Ray Tube used for television and computer screens.

CSG   See **constructive solid geometry**.

Culling   The action of identifying and removing objects from a view of a scene.

Cyberspace   A popular name given to the virtual 3D domain.

Database   A collection of related records organized such that particular classes of records are easily accessed.

Deep sensations   Measure pressure and pain. using receptors deep within body tissue.

Depth buffer   See **z-buffer**.

Depth cues   Strategies used by the brain to estimate depth.

Depth of field   The distance over which an in-focus image is created in a lens.

Digitizer   A system for capturing 2D or 3D Cartesian coordinates.

dVISE   Division's virtual world simulation and authoring software tool.

dVS   Division's VR runtime environment.

Dynamic constraints   Physical constraints associated with moving objects such as mass and inertia.

Dynamic vertices   Vertices that can change their position in a VE.

Eardrum   A thin membrane in the middle ear that moves in sympathy with incoming sound pressure waves.

Edge   A line formed where two polygons meet.

Elastic collisions   Are associated with colliding rigid objects.

Environment mapping   A rendering technique where background reflections are seen in an object's surface.

Ergonomics   Using human dimensions in a design process.

Exoskeleton   An articulated structure surrounding part of our body to measure joint angles.

External sound stage   Externalizing sound sources outside our head.

Exteroceptive sensations   Touch sensations detected over our body surface.

Extruding   A modeling technique where a 2D cross-section is used to create a 3D volume.

Eye convergence   The ability to rotate our eyes and focus upon an object.

Eye divergence   The action of moving both eyes outwards.

Eye relief   The distance between the user's face and the optics of a HMD.

Eye tracking   The technique of monitoring the gaze direction of the eye.

FEA   See **finite element analysis**.

FFD   See **free-form deformation**.

Field   The odd or even lines of a video frame.

Field of view (FOV)   The largest solid angle where incident light can form an image.

File   A collection of related data.

Finite element analysis (FEA) A technique for simulating dynamic stresses in an object.

Fixating The deliberate action of gazing at a point in space.

Flat screen view A VE displayed in a window on a computer screen.

Flat shading A process where a polygon is shaded with a single color.

Flicker Occurs when an image is not refreshed fast enough.

Flight simulator A VE for training and evaluating pilots.

Flying The action of moving from part of the VE to another.

Force feedback Applying forces to the user's fingers, arm or shoulder.

FOV See **field of view**.

Fovea The high-resolution central zone in the retina.

Frame Two fields of a video image, or a single rendering of a 3D world.

Frame store A memory device for storing one video frame.

Free-form deformation (FFD) A technique for distorting 2D and 3D objects.

Front face The side of a polygon containing the surface normal.

Fusion frequency The frequency when a flashing image appears continuous to the human visual system.

Gaze direction The viewer's eye direction.

Generator A computer program that creates VRML files. Synonymous with authoring tools.

Geometry A description of the shape of an object and its surface characteristics.

Gesture recognition The recognition of hand gestures made by the VR user.

Gouraud shading A shading technique that interpolates color over a surface.

Graphical user interface (GUI) A graphics-based user interface.

Graph plotter A device for creating line-based drawings.

Graphic primitive A shape or object used by a graphic system to construct more complex scenes.

GUI See **graphical user interface**.

Hand tracking The action of monitoring the position and orientation of the human hand.

Haptic Synonomous with touch and force.

Head mounted display (HMD) A display system attached to the user's head.

Head related transfer functions (HRTFs)   Encode the physical influence the upper torso have on incoming sound pressure waves.

Head tracking   The action of monitoring the position and orientation of a human head.

Heave   The vertical translation of a motion platform.

Hidden-surface removal   A rendering strategy for removing invisible or masked surfaces.

HMD   See **head mount display**.

HRTF   See **head related transfer functions**.

HSV   Hue, Saturation and Value color model.

HTML   HyperText Markup Language. A file specification supporting hyperlinks.

Hue   The attribute given to a color that describes its relative position within the visible spectrum.

Human factors   The issues pertaining to human behavior such as sight, sound, touch and equilibrium.

Hyperlink   A reference to a URL that is associated with an Anchor node

Hz   Means cycles/second. Named after the scientist Hertz.

IG   See **image generator**.

Iggo dome receptor   Touch receptors with a slow rate of adaptation.

Illumination model   Describes how light is emitted, reflected, transmitted and absorbed within a virtual world.

Image generator (IG)   A computer capable of rendering real-time images.

Image plane   Synonymous with the picture plane.

Immersion   The sensation of being part of a VE.

Immersive VR   A VR system where the user is immersed with a VE through the use of an immersive display

Instance   A reference to a master object.

Interactive computer graphics   A computer interface that supports real-time, two-way, graphical interaction.

Interactive glove   A glove that monitors finger and hand gestures.

Internal sound stage   The internalization of a sound source.

Internet   The world-wide named network of computers that communicate with each other using a common set of communication protocols known as TCP/IP.

Inter-ocular distance   The distance between the optical centers of our eyes.

Interpenetrating objects When one virtual object intersects another.

Intranet A private network that uses the same protocols and standards as the Internet.

Inverse Kinematics Modeling the movement of a jointed limb, such as an arm or leg.

I/O An acronym for Input/Output.

Iris The pigmented, opaque circular structure positioned in front of the eye's lens.

Joystick A device for monitoring hand movements.

JPEG Joint Photographic Experts Group.

Lag See **latency**.

Laparoscopic simulator A training simulator for 'key-hole' surgery.

Laparoscopy Surgery undertaken through small incisions in the side of the body.

Latency The time delay (or lag) between activating a process and its termination.

LCD See **liquid crystal display**.

LED See **light emitting diode**.

Level of detail (LOD) The amount of detail or complexity displayed in a scene.

Light adaptation When the eye adjusts to a bright environment, having been adapted to low light levels.

Light emitting diode (LED) A semiconductor device that emits light on the application of a voltage.

Light source A virtual source of illumination used by the renderer to calculate light levels on a surface.

Liquid crystal display (LCD) Employs liquid crystals whose molecules can be oriented to different positions by the application of an electric field.

Macula Hair cells in the utricle within the vestibular system for sensing gravity.

Material A definition of the surface characteristics of an object, such as color, shininess, texture and transparency.

Meissner's corpuscles Receptors for measuring touch sensations in the fingertips.

MIDI Musical Instrument Digital Interface. A standard for digital music representation.

MIME Multipurpose Internet Mail Extension. Used to specify file typing rules for Internet applications including browsers.

Model A geometric representation of an object produced by a CAD system or 3D modeling package.

Model board A scale model of an airport used before the introduction of VEs.

Modeling   The action of building a VE.

Momentum   The product of mass and velocity.

Monochrome   The use of one color as in black and white photography.

Monocular   Using one eye.

Monocular depth cues   Mechanisms such as motion parallax for estimating depth with one eye.

Motion parallax   A monocular visual cue for estimating the depth of moving objects.

Motion platform   A moving platform associated with simulators.

Motion sickness   Unpleasant symptoms experienced when the brain receives conflicting visual and motion cues.

Mouse   A pointing device used for controlling a screen's cursor.

MPEG   Moving Picture Experts Group.

Multimedia   An integrated computer presentation including graphics, audio, text and video.

Network   A set of interconnected computers.

Node   The basic component of a scene graph.

NTSC   National Television Standards Convention is a television standard widely used in the U.S.A.

Object constancy   The way objects in the real world appear stationary when we move our heads.

Object picking   The action of selecting an object in a VE.

Object space   The coordinate system in which an object is defined.

Optic nerve   Connects the eye to the brain.

Orthogonal   At right angles to some datum.

Ossicular system   A system of small bones in the inner ear.

Pacinian corpuscles   Touch receptors used for detecting vibrations.

PAL   Television standard used in the UK and other countries.

Palette   A collection of colors.

Paradigm   A pattern or model.

Parallax   The apparent movement of an object arising from a change in the position of the observer.

Particle system   A collection of discrete particles used to model natural phenomena.

Percentile One of 99 actual or notional values of a variable dividing its distribution into 100 groups with equal frequencies.

Peripheral vision Visual information detected at the periphery of our field of view.

Persistence of vision The eye's ability to record a visual signal after the stimulus has been removed.

Perspective depth cues Size cues that enable us to estimate depth.

Phong shading A shading technique that introduces reflective highlights into a surface.

Photopic vision Vision with the use of cone receptors.

Photopsin A protein used in cone receptors.

Photorealism Highly realistic computer-generated scenes.

Photoreceptors The rods and cones that convert light into nerve signals.

Physical simulation Algorithms for simulating physical behavior.

Picking See **object picking**.

Picture plane A projection plane used to capture an image, especially for perspective projections.

Pinna The outer part of the ear.

Pitch The rotational angle about a horizontal x-axis, orthogonal to the forward-facing z-axis.

Pixel The smallest addressable picture element on a display.

Planar polygon Has its vertices in one plane.

PNG Portable Network Graphics. A specification for representing 2D images in files.

Point-and-fly A command to initiate a flying direction and action.

Pointing device A hardware device connected to the user's computer by which the user directly controls the location and direction of the pointer.

Polygon A shape bounded by straight edges.

Polygonal mesh A boundary structure formed from a collection polygons.

Polyhedron An object having a polygonal boundary.

Polyline A chain of straight line segments.

Portal A virtual 'doorway' into another VE.

Presence The sense of realism created by being immersed in a VE.

Properties   The attributes associated with an object such as color, position and
behavior.

Proprioceptive sensations   Monitor the status of the body, such as position,
equilibrium and muscles.

Radiosity   A global illumination model for computing light intensities resulting from
multiple diffuse reflections.

RAM   An acronym for Random Access Memory.

Raster   One line of a frame or field.

Ray tracing   Uses the geometry of light rays to render a scene.

Real time   An instantaneous reaction to any changes in signals being processed.

Refresh rate   The frequency a raster display refreshes its screen.

Renderer
(a) **Image**: A program for creating a shaded 3D image.

(b) **Acoustic**: A program for simulating sound patterns in a VE.

Rendering   The process of projecting a 3D object onto a 2D display, clipping it to fit
the view, removing hidden surfaces and shading the visible ones according to the
light sources.

Resolution   A measure of a system's ability to record fine detail.

RGB   Red, Green and Blue. A color space where a color is represented as a
combination of the primary colors red, green and blue.

Rhodopsin   Light-sensitive pigment found in rod receptors.

Rigid body   An object whose geometry is fixed.

Rods   Light receptors in the retina that are active in dim lighting conditions.

Roll angle   The angle of rotation about the forward-facing heading vector.

Ruffini's end organs   Touch receptors in deep tissue that do not adapt to any extent.

Saturation   The purity of a color in terms of the white light component and the color
component.

Scaling matrix   Changes the size of an object.

Scanner   An input device for converting photographs into a digital form.

Scene graph   An ordered collection of nodes as used in VRML.

Scotopic vision   Rod or night vision.

Scotopsin   A protein found in rhodopsin that aids the conversion of light into
electricity.

Scripting language A computer language that is interpreted and executed sequentially.

Semicircular canals The anterior, posterior and horizontal ducts in the vestibular system for predicting loss off equilibrium.

Shading The process of coloring an object.

Soft objects Objects modeled from mathematical equations.

Somatic senses The senses of touch, pain, position and temperature.

Spaceball A 6DOF pointing device manufactured by Spaceball Technologies, Inc.

Spatialized sound Sound filtered so that it seems to be localized in 3D space.

Stereocilla Small hairs in the vestibular system for monitoring head position.

Stereogram An image that contains parallax information, such as random dot stereograms.

Stereopsis The action of obtaining two views of an object with two eyes.

Stereoscope A device for creating a stereoscopic image from a pair of images containing parallax information.

Stereoscopic Requires two images with parallax information, giving the illusion of depth and relief.

Surface attributes Qualities such as color and texture.

Surface of revolution See **swept surface**.

Surface patch A surface description that can be used to form a complex surface.

Surge The forward movement of a motion platform.

Sway The horizontal movement of a motion platform.

Swept surface A 3D surface formed by rotating a contour about an axis.

Tactile feedback Sensory information detected through the sense of touch.

Tactile receptors Measure sensations of touch.

TCP/IP Transport Control Protocol/Internet Protocol is a networking protocol used for communications between computers. TCP provides the transport layer of the ISO OSI (Open Systems Interconnect) model. IP provides the network layer.

Teleporting The action of moving from one position in a VE to another.

Telepresence Relaying a view of a scene back to some distant viewer.

Texture map A 2D pattern image for use as surface decoration.

Texture mapping Substituting detail stored within a texture map onto a surface.

Toolkit   A software system for building, visualizing and interacting with VEs.

Torque   A rotational force.

Tracking   Monitoring an object's 3D position and orientation.

Triangulation   Reducing a shape into a triangular mesh.

Update rate   The rate at which a process is modified.

URL   Uniform Resource Locator.

Value   Is equivalent to the term lightness.

VE   See **virtual environment**.

Vertex   The end of an edge.

Vestibular system   Monitors the body's acceleration, equilibrium and relationship with the earth's gravitational field.

Virtual domain   The imaginary space inside a computer.

Virtual environment (VE)   A 3D data set describing an environment based upon real-world or abstract objects and data.

Virtual hand   A simple model of a hand built into the VE.

Virtual reality (VR)   A generic term for systems that create a real-time visual/audio/haptic experience.

Virtual world   See **world**.

Visceral sensations   Record discomfort or pain from the viscera organs in the chest cavity.

Visual acuity   The eye's ability to discern fine detail.

Visual cortex   Part of the brain used for processing visual information.

Visual cues   Signals or prompts derived from a scene.

Vomit center   Part of the brain responsible for initiating vomiting.

VR   An acronym for Virtual Reality.

VRML   Virtual Reality Modeling Language.

VRML browser   See **browser**.

VRML file   A set of VRML nodes and statements as defined in ISO/IEC 14772.

Wand   A pointing device that moves in 3D and that enables a user to indicate aposition in the 3D coordinate system.

Widgets   Graphical user interface controls such as menus and dialog boxes.

Wire frame A 3D object where all edges are drawn, producing a 'see through' wire-like image.

World A collection of one or more VRML files and other multimedia content that, when interpreted by a VRML browser, presents an interactive experience to the user.

World coordinate space The Cartesian coordinate system used for locating 3D worlds.

World Wide Web The collection of documents, data and content typically encoded in HTML pages and accessible via the Internet using the HTTP protocol.

Yaw angle A angle of rotation about a vertical axis.

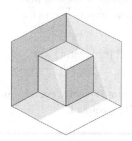

Appendix A
VRML Web sites

Introduction

The following are useful Web sites for VRML VEs.

http://193.49.43.3/dif/3D_crystals.html
http://amber.rc.arizona.edu/
http://fluo.univ-lemans.fr:8001/vrml/vrml.html
http://hiway.net/~crispen/vrml/viewing.html
http://home.netscape.com/eng/live3d/
http://home.netscape.com/comprod/products/-
     navigator/version_2.0/plugins/vrml_sites.html
http://infopark.newcollege.edu:80/vrmLab/warehouse
http://nssdc.gsfc.nasa.gov/cohoweb/vrml.coho.html
http://overlord.nrl.navy.mil/vrml/vrml.html
http://pentium.intel.com/procs/ppro/intro/
http://piano.symgrp.com/playbill/
http://reality.sgi.com/employees/cmarrin_engr/vrml/
http://vag.vrml.org/www-vrml/
http://virtual_business.labs.bt.com/vrml/portal/home/
http://vrml.sgi.com/cafe/
http://vrml.sgi.com/worlds/vrml2/
http://vrml.sgi.com/intro.html
http://vs.sony.co.jp/
http://vs.spiw.com/vs/
http://vwww.com/
http://weblynx.com.au/virtual.htm
http://webspace.sgi.com/worlds/overview.html
http://www.3dconstruction.com/
http://www.3dweb.com/
http://www.3name3d.com/

http://www.acuris.com/
http://www.aritek.com/vrml.html
http://www.aereal.com/instant/
http://www.austin.ibm.com/vrml/
http://www.aw.sgi.com/
http://www.bentley.com/vrml
http://www.blacksun.com/
http://www.brlabs.com/
http://www.calgari.com/calgari/index.html
http://www.calagari.com/products/ts3/ts3_feat.html
http://www.calpoly.edu/~bsmith/c3vrml.html
http://www.cgrg.ohio-state.edu/
http://www.chaco.com/
http://www.cica.indiana.edu/graphics/3D.objects.html
http://www.communities.com/
http://www.construct.net/
http://www.coryphaeus.com/
http://www.cosmosoftware.com/
http://www.crg.cs.nott.ac.uk/~dns/vr/
http://www.cybertown.com/
http://www.dimensionx.com/
http://www.dur.ac.uk/~dcs3py/pages/wok/-Documents/VR-Survey/index.html
http://www.eagen.com/home.html
http://www.eagen.com/warpspace/index.html
http://www.eleccafe.com/
http://www.eritek.com/
http://www.hash.com/
http://www.idt.ntnu.no~oleholt/holoen1.htm
http://www.ids-net.com/ids/vrml/explore.html
http://www.ids-net.com/ids/vrml/splitlnk.html
http://www.ids-net.com/ids/vrealm.html
http://www.iicm.edu/vrml
http://www.iion.com/Winternet.vrml/
http://www.immersive.com/
http://www.inquiry.com/techtips/vrml_pro/
http://www.insead.fr/Encyclopedia/Computer-Sciences/VR/vrml.htm
http://www.intervista.com/
http://www.isinet.com/MAX/vrml/struct.html
http://www.itl.nist.gov/div894/ovrt/OVRThome.html
http://www.itl.nist.gov/div894/ovrt/projects/vrml/-vrmlfilesw.html
http://www.itm.pt/frames/itmtrek/vrml.htm
http://www.ktx.com/
http://www.landform.com/landform.htm
http://www.lightscape.com/
http://www.lookup.com/Homepages/56215/vrml/-list.html

http://www.macromedia.com/
http://www.marketcentral.com/
http://www.marketcentral.com/vrml/vrml.html
http://www.mcp.com/general/foundry/
http://www.micrografx.com/simply3d/
http://www.mindworkshop.com/alchemy/alchemy.html
http://www.mpic-tueb.mpg.de/projects/-vrtueb/vrtueb.html
http://www.msc.cornell.edu/~houle/Stars/
http://www.mtv.com/
http://www.multigen.com/
http://www.nba.com/knicks/
http://www.ncsa.uiuc.edu/General/VRML/-VRMLHome.html
http://www.neuro.sfc.keio.ac.jp/~aly/polygon/vrml/ika/
http://www.newcollege.edu/vrmLab/Frames/
http://www.newtek.com/3d/3danim.html
http://www.nis.za/intershop/creative.html
http://www. nist.gov/
http://www.northplains.com/
http://www.nssdc.gsfc.nasa.gov/cohoweb/vrml/coho.html
http://www.nyse.com/
http://www.nytimes.com/
http://www.nyu.edu/
http://www.nyu.edu/pages/mathmol/library/-library.html
http://www.nyu.edu/pages/scivis/
http://www.ocnus.com/models
http://www.oz-inc.com/ov/download/index.html
http://www.pacificnet.net/~mediastorm/
http://www.paradigmsim.com/
http://www.paragraph.com/
http://www.paragraph.com/products/i3dfamily/-SpaceBuilder
http://www.pc.chenie.th-darmstadt.de/vrml/
http://www.photomodeler.com/ http://www.radiance.com/Ez3d-VRPro.html
http://www.planet9.com/vrsoma.html
http://www.radiance.com/
http://www.radiance.com/Ez3d-VRPro.html
http://www.realimation.com/
http://www.rlspace.com/
http://www.ru.paragraph.com/
http://www.sense8.com/
http://www.sgi.com/
http://www.snafu.de~hg/
http://www.soho-ny.com/index.html
http://www.squirrel.com.au/virtualreality/-vrpackroma.html
http://www.strata3d.com/
http://www.superscape.com/

http://www.stl.nps.navy.mil/~auv/
http://www.tcc.iz.net/~jeffs/vrmLab/
http://www.terravirtual.com/
http://www.thevertex.com/
http://www.tristero.com/coffee/vrcoffee/
http://www.virtpark.com/theme/factinfo.html
http://www.virtuocity.com/
http://www.virtus.com/index.html
http://www.vream.com/
http://www.vrml.org/VRML1.0/vrml/10c.html
http://www.vrml.org/VRML2.0/FINAL/
http://www.vrml.sgi.com/tools/
http://www.vrmlsite.com/
http://www.vrnz.co.nz/
http://www.vr-publishing.com/
http://www.vruniverse.com/
http://www.ywd.com/cindy/texture.html
http://www.well.com/user/caferace/vrml.html
http://www.worlds.net/

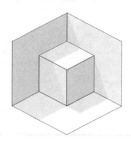

Appendix B
HMDs

Introduction

The following table identifies some HMDs currently available.

Name	Resolution [h x v]	Overlap	FOV
Cyber Eye	230 × 420		22.5°h × 16.8°v
Cyberface 2	319 × 117	60.6°	140°h
Cyberface 3	720 × 240	N/A	80°h
Eyegen 3	493 × 250	Variable	40° at 100% overlap
Flight Helmet	240 × 120	79%	90°-100°h
HRX	416 × 277	65°	106°h × 75°v
MRG 2	240 × 240	N/A	84°h × 65°v
NASA Ames CRT	400 lines	90°	120°h per eye
NASA Ames View	640 × 220	90°	120°h
Quaterwave	1280 × 1024		50°h
WFOV	1280 × 1024	40°	80-110°h × 60°v
HMSI 1000	450 × 220	100%	65°h × 46°v
VIM 1000pv	800 × 225	67% 100%	100°h × 30°v
Datavisor 80	1280 × 1024	50%	80° per eye
Stereo Viewer-1	1280 × 960	100%	57° circular

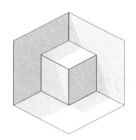

Appendix C
Trackers

Introduction

The following table identifies some trackers currently available.

Product	Tech.	Positional Accuracy	Positional Resolution	Angular Accuracy	Angular Resolution
ADL-1	M	0.2"	0.025"		
BOOM	M	0.16"			0.1°
Logitech	A	0.004"	0.004"	0.1°	0.1°
Digisonic	A		<0.005"		0.1°
Ascension	E	0.1°	0.03"	0.5°	0.1° at 12"
Polhemus Isotrak II	E	0.1" at <30"	0.0015"	0.75° at <30"	0.1°
Polhemus Fastrak	E	0.03" at <30"	0.002"	0.15° at <30"	0.05°
UNC	O		<2mm		<2°
ELITE	O	1/24,000 of FOV	1/65,536 of FOV		
Wayfinder-VR	I			±2°	±1°
Vector 2X	I			2°	2°
TCM2	I			±0.5° to ±1.5°	0.1°

Technology key: E = Electromagnetic I = Inertial
                 M = Mechanical   O = Optical
                 A = Acoustic

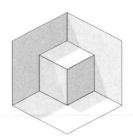

Appendix D
VRML program

Introduction

This VRML 1.0 program listing is part of the VRML document located at: http://www.vrml.org/VRML1.0/vrml10c.html.

```
#VRML V1.0 test
Separator {
   Separator {      # Simple track-light geometry:
      Translation { translation 0 4 0 }
      Separator {
         Material { emissiveColor 0.1 0.3 0.3 }
         Cube {
            width   0.1
            height  0.1
            depth   4
         }
      }
      Rotation { rotation 0 1 0  1.57079 }
      Separator {
         Material { emissiveColor 0.3 0.1 0.3 }
         Cylinder {
            radius  0.1
            height  .2
         }
      }
      Rotation { rotation -1 0 0  1.57079 }
      Separator {
         Material { emissiveColor 0.3 0.3 0.1 }
         Rotation { rotation 1 0 0  1.57079 }
```

```
         Translation { translation 0 -.2 0 }
         Cone {
            height  .4
            bottomRadius .2
         }
         Translation { translation 0 .4 0 }
         Cylinder {
            radius  0.02
            height  .4
         }
      }
   }
   SpotLight {      # Light from above
      location 0 4 0
      direction 0 -1 0
      intensity     0.9
      cutOffAngle    0.7
   }
   Separator {     # Wall geometry; just three flat polygons
      Coordinate3 {
         point [
            -2 0 -2, -2 0 2, 2 0 2, 2 0 -2,
            -2 4 -2, -2 4 2, 2 4 2, 2 4 -2]
      }
      IndexedFaceSet {
         coordIndex [ 0, 1, 2, 3, -1,
               0, 4, 5, 1, -1,
               0, 3, 7, 4, -1
               ]
      }
   }
   WWWAnchor {   # A hyper-linked cow:
      name "http://www.foo.edu/CowProject/AboutCows.html"
      Separator {
         Translation { translation 0 1 0 }
         WWWInline {   # Reference another object
            name "http://www.foo.edu/3DObjects/cow.wrl"
         }
      }
   }
}
```

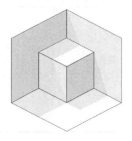

Appendix E
Web sites for VR products

Introduction

The following sites are worth visiting to obtain more information about VR hardware and software products.

Cadcentre	www.cadcentre.com
Division	www.division.com
Dreamality Technologies	www.dreamalitytechnologies.com
Evans & Sutherland	www.es.com
Fakespace	www.fakespace.com
James Hans	dspace.dial.pipex.com/david_hans
Lake DSP Pty.	www.lakedsp.com
Motion Analysis Corporation	www.motionanalysis.com
Polhemus	www.polhemus.com
Pyramid Systems	www.pyramidsystems.com
Sense8	www.sense8.com
Silicon Graphics	www.sgi.com
Spacetec IM	www.spacetec.com
Stereographics	www.stereographics.com
Superscape	www.superscape.com
Teesside University	www.teesside.ac.uk
Transom Corporation	www.transom.com
Trimension	www.trimension-inc.com
Viewpoint DataLabs	www.viewpoint.com
Virtual Presence	www.vrweb.com
Virtual Research	www.virtualresearch.com

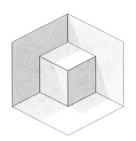

References

Blinn J.F. and Newell M.E. (1976) Texture and reflection in computer generated imagse. *Comm. ACM*, **19**, 542–547.

Blinn J.F. (1978) Simulation of Wrinkled Surfaces. *SIGGRAPH 78*, 286-292.

Gouraud H. (1971) Computer display of curved surfaces. *PhD Thesis*, University of Utah.

Guyton A.C. (1991) *Textbook of Medical Physiology*. Philadelphia: W.B. Saunders Company.

Hartman J. and Wernecke J. (1996) *The VRML 2.0 Handbook: Building Moving Worlds on the Web*, Addison-Wesley.

Hollands R. (1995) Sourceless trackers. *VR News*, **4**(3), 23–29.

Julesz B. (1971) *Foundations of Cyclopean Perception*, University of Chicago Press.

Kamat V.V. (1993) A survey of Techniques for Simulation of Dynamic Collision Detection and Response. *Computers and Graphics* **17**(4), 379–385.

Phong B. (1973) Illumination for computer generated images. *PhD Thesis*, University of Utah; also in *Comm. ACM*, **18**, 311–317.

Plenge G. (1974) On the difference between localization and lateralization. *Journal of the Acoustics Society of America*, **56**, 944–951.

Shaw E.A.G. (1974) The external ear. In *Handbook of Sensory Physiology*. (Keidel W.D. and Neff W.D., eds.). New York: Springer-Verlag.

Sutherland I.E. (1965) The ultimate display. *Proceedings of the IFIP Congress* **2**, 506–508.

Vince J.A. (1995) *Virtual Reality Systems*, Wokingham: Addison-Wesley.

Williams L. (1983) Pyramidal Parametrics. *SIGGRAPH 83* 1–11.

Tidwell M., Johnston R.S., Melville D., Furness T.A. III (1995) The virtual retinal display – A retinal scanning imaging system. *Proceedings of Virtual Reality World* 325–334.

Index